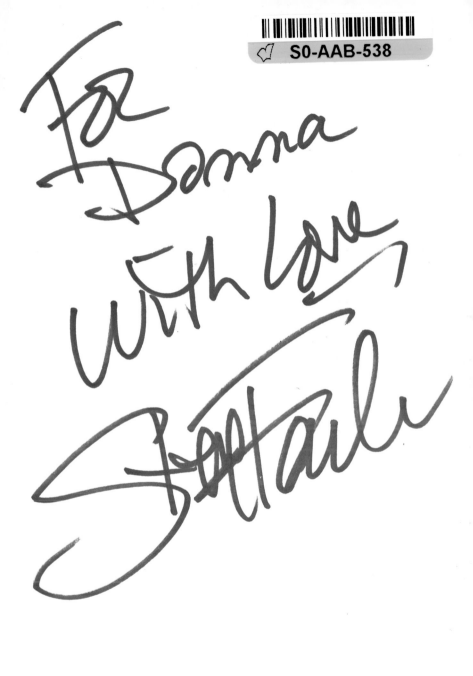

For Donna
With love

THE
Radical Leap
RE-ENERGIZED

THE
Radical Leap
RE-ENERGIZED

STEVE FARBER

PUBLISHING

For information on distribution rights, royalties, derivative works or licensing opportunities on behalf of this content or work, please contact the publisher at the address below or via email, info@nolimitpublishinggroup.com.

COMPANIES, ORGANIZATIONS, INSTITUTIONS, AND INDUSTRY PUBLICATIONS: Quantity discounts are available on bulk purchases of this book for reselling, educational purposes, subscription incentives, gifts, sponsorship, or fundraising. Special books or book excerpts can also be created to fit specific needs such as private labeling with your logo on the cover and a message from a VIP printed inside. Contact chris@nolimitpublishinggroup.com or call 480-269-3350.

No Limit Publishing Group
No Limit Enterprises
560 Carlsbad Village Drive Suite 202
Carlsbad, CA 92008
info@nolimitpublishinggroup.com

This book was printed in the United States of America

PRAISE FOR *THE RADICAL LEAP RE-ENERGIZED*

"Today's world demands a different leader: one who has the heart and courage to change it for the better. If you're ready to be one of them, read this phenomenal book and succeed."
—**Darren Hardy**, publisher *SUCCESS* magazine, bestselling author *The Compound Effect*

"With his strikingly original voice and unparalleled storytelling ability, Steve Farber brings us *The Radical Leap Re-Energized*. This edgy leadership parable not only entertains and inspires, it teaches us how to become great leaders and change the world in the bargain. We wholeheartedly encourage you to take the LEAP!"
—**Jim Kouzes and Barry Posner**, authors of the bestselling *The Leadership Challenge and Credibility*

"*The Radical Leap Re-Energized* is a clarion call for 21st century leaders and those who aspire to be. The LEAP will stay with me and will be required reading for leaders in my organization."
—**Tony Uphoff**, CEO, UBM TechWeb

"Steve Farber's work is even more important and more useful today than when it first appeared on the scene."
—**Tom Peters**, International bestselling author of *In Search of Excellence*

"Steve Farber has captured the heart of leadership in this wonderful book. If you'd really love to make a difference in this world, read it and apply its lessons to your life and business."

—**Rita Davenport**, former President,
Arbonne International

"Rejuvenate and revitalize with Farber's amazing *The Radical Leap Re-Energized*. It is timeless, universal, and extremely useful—and it will catapult you to success!"

—**Marshall Goldsmith**, author of the
New York Times bestsellers, *MOJO* and
What Got You Here Won't Get You There

"There are two types of well-written leadership books: GOOD ones that you read once and pass along to a few friends, or GREAT ones that you read over and over and give to as many people as you can. *The Radical Leap Re-Energized* is one of the GREAT ones, and it is a total game-changer."

—**Tommy Spaulding**, author of the *New York Times*
bestseller, *It's Not Just Who You Know*

"Steve Farber's books are as easy and enjoyable to read as they are insightful. This volume will be a great addition to any leader's library."

—**Patrick Lencioni**, President, The Table Group,
author, *The Five Dysfunctions of a Team*

"Steve Farber's masterwork, *The Radical Leap Re-Energized*, is an inspired opus on what it means to be a leader of substance and significance. You'll find yourself coming back to it again and again."

—**Michael E. Ventling**, Global CFO, Ernst & Young

"If you want to lead as big as you dream, Farber can take you to the extreme. This book is your path to soaring success."

—**Tim Sanders**, former Chief Solutions Officer at Yahoo!, author, *Today We Are Rich*

"A business fable that will stick with you, and, if you push yourself, help you take the leap."

—**Seth Godin**, author, *Linchpin*

"A brilliantly captivating book, vibrant and audacious, and an absolute joy to read. Every bit as engaging as Steve Farber himself."

—**Sally Hogshead**, speaker and author of *Fascinate: Your 7 Triggers to Persuasion and Captivation*

"Steve Farber leaps again. I was into it the first time. This time, I'm *leaping* with him!"

—**Chris Brogan**, President, Human Business Works.

"I have read most leadership books in print. None have resonated more than this one. It is timeless, relevant and energizing and should be required reading for all business leaders of the 21st century."

—**Pamela Slim**, author, *Escape from Cubicle Nation: From Corporate Prisoner to Thriving Entrepreneur*

"I've read the original *Radical Leap* over a dozen times, and year after year, experience after experience, I have found that the concepts hold fast and true. *The Radical Leap Re-Energized* kickstarts and expands the experience to the next level. This really is a masterpiece."

—**Burton M. Goldfield**, President and CEO, TriNet

I dedicate this book to the memory of Bill Foster, who did what he loved in the service of others and left us too soon—physically, at least. He was an Extreme Leader who flew high and loved deep.

We miss him.

■ CONTENTS

■ FOREWORD

There is no higher calling than building a team in order to solve a meaningful and difficult challenge. Most great teams are driven by great leaders. However, leadership is not about organizational structure or hierarchy; it's about getting people to follow and be excited by the mission. Steve Farber's *The Radical Leap Re-Energized* examines the very definition of leadership and explores what makes someone not just a good leader, but an Extreme Leader.

The earlier version of this book, *The Radical Leap*, was a gift from a colleague. I'll never forget the way he presented it to me... "Burton!" he said, "it looks like somebody stole a bunch of your ideas and put them in a wonderful book!" I laughed, accepted the book and read it that very night. Since then, I've read it over a dozen times, and each time it puts a smile on my face. Year after year, experience after experience, I have found that the concepts in this book hold true. In fact, Steve's articulations of these important issues clarify why I'm excited to get up in the morning and pursue my dreams related to building teams.

When I first read this book, I was struck by how closely its philosophy on building a successful company mirrored my own experiences in companies like Rational Software, Hyperion and IBM. That is why, when I joined TriNet as the President and CEO, *The Radical Leap* was my first selection for the TriNet book club, and Steve was the keynote speaker at our 2010 national sales meeting. I see Steve as the gold standard in leadership coaching due to his clear articulation of the challenges and opportunities that a leader faces, and I am honored to have Steve as a special advisor to TriNet.

At TriNet we are privileged to have as our clients 7,000 small businesses that are fighting against all odds to build companies that are making the world a better place. Many of them are focused on life's important issues: curing cancer and other challenging diseases, cleaning our water and air, creating the next generation of software products and services, as well as innovative non-profits that span the globe. I am in awe of the many inspiring solutions our clients are delivering.

Take Muhammed Chaudhry, an advocate for improving science and math education in our public schools; he built up the Silicon Valley Education Foundation from scratch. There's also Gary Swart of oDesk, who is creating a borderless economy by connecting employers with an on-demand global workforce. And Maureen Taylor of SNP, who is improving the way leaders communicate to all stakeholders. There are thousands more. The innovation that is coming out of the companies we work with is improving the quality of life across our planet. They are the exemplars of Extreme Leadership.

The Extreme Leadership that Steve writes about comes down to this: leadership is important not only because it impacts the lives of the teams we build, but also the lives of our customers, and ultimately, the state of the world we live in. Additionally, leadership is not about positional authority, but about how we can create an environment where every person in the company believes he or she is a leader and rises to the challenge. In this paradigm, all colleagues understand their own importance and have the primary data to make decisions that will ultimately make a better company. The result is colleagues feel a natural instinct to come forward with great ideas. So in the end, I believe the best corporate cultures are the ones where leadership is shared, and the best ideas win.

Difficult market conditions, such as the ones we are experiencing today, make the lessons in this wonderful book more important—and challenging—than ever. Steve points out how difficult it is to be a good leader. If it were formulaic, everybody would do it. But it's not a formula; there is something elusive and extraordinary about it. Something extreme.

Ultimately, I believe in the power of businesses small and large to create jobs, drive economic growth and build a better world, and to do that we need more of the extreme kind of leaders that Steve describes. I encourage you to read this book cover to cover. And don't worry, even though this is challenging stuff, it is not dogma, nor is it preachy; it's accessible, entertaining, and fun. You don't have to wade through a lot of business buzzwords to pull out one or two life-changing ideas.

I hope this book speaks to you the way it has spoken to me. Enjoy the reading!

–**Burton M. Goldfield**
President and CEO
TriNet Group, Inc.

■ INTRODUCTION

I've always considered myself to be a business guy. Having started out as an entrepreneur in my late 20s to early 30s, I've worked for the last two decades in leadership development in the corporate world. I spent six years as vice president of The Tom Peters Company, whose founder and namesake is arguably the most influential management guru of our time. In addition to Tom, I count among my mentors Jim Kouzes and Barry Posner, co-creators of the legendary *Leadership Challenge* books and the phenomenal research behind them. The business world has been my laboratory, my university, my playground, and a major part of my personal, social fabric. I've had exposure to or worked with just about every kind of business and industry you can imagine.

Again: *business guy*.

So, when the first version of this book was published under the title, *The Radical Leap: A Personal Lesson in Extreme Leadership*, I was proud to see it featured as a Reader's Choice Award winner in *Fast Company* magazine and displayed in the management sections of retail and airport bookstores around the country. In 2009, when it was listed in Covert and Sattersten's *The 100 Best Business Books of All Time*, right next to Tom's *In Search of Excellence* and Jim and Barry's *The Leadership Challenge*, well, to say that blew my mind would rank among the 100 biggest understatements of all time.

I've been deeply gratified and, to be honest, more than a little surprised by the business world's warm reception to *Leap*.

But the biggest surprises have had little to do with business, per se.

Over the short years since *Leap*'s first publication, I've heard from principals, schoolteachers and students; pastors, rabbis and clergy people of all stripes; bloggers and social media mavens; volunteer workers and nonprofit missionaries who've reached out to me to say that the ideas and inspiration in this book have helped them excel as leaders and succeed in changing their pieces of the world for the better. And several of these people, I'm grateful to say, I now count among my dearest friends.

In other words, it turns out that *The Radical Leap* wasn't just a business book, after all.

The Radical Leap Re-Energized represents a relaunch and a recommitment to a universal set of life-changing/world-changing ideas. This new incarnation is actually two books, *The Radical Leap* and *The Radical Edge*, woven together into a new, expanded, and rejuvenated work. Even though I originally wrote it in two separate endeavors, this full story is, in retrospect, the way it was always meant to be.

I didn't make these ideas up—I think you'll find that they're timeless and universal—but I did make up the story surrounding them.

This book is a novel—a parable, so to speak. I've taken broad, creative license with the story and the characters in it in order to create an entertaining delivery system for ideas and practices that are anything but fictional.

Part One: The Radical Leap offers a foundation, an operating system, for Extreme Leadership, and Part Two: The Radical Edge, takes it deeper with some significant, personal applications and calls to action.

This book will take you a few hours to read and a lifetime to practice. If you do, my hope is that you'll strive to do what you love in the service of people who love what you do; that you'll become the walking, talking, living, breathing example of Extreme Leadership in action.

That, I believe, is how individually and collectively we're going to have a real shot at changing the world for the better, in business and beyond.

"I may not have the capacity to love everyone, but I do have the capacity to act as if I do and run my business accordingly."

—Agnes Golden

Part One:
The Radical Leap

Tuesday

■ O N E

In one respect, at least, I'm a creature of habit. Every day I'm in town, I head for the waterfront. Which is why, I realize now, it had been easy for him to find me.

It was another one of those typical San Diego days, the sky was blue and bright, and the ocean was sparkling as it slapped its waves onto the shores of Mission Beach. I was sitting on the seawall and watching the scenery walk, run, skate, and cycle by on the boardwalk. Here was the epitome of beach culture, beautifully sculpted people gathered together for the top-end of the gene pool convention. This world, with its high tattoo and body piercing to square inch of flesh ratio, was very different from the corporate world I, as a leadership consultant, worked in every day. That's why I loved living here, it kept me lively. I lifted my face to the sun, closed my eyes behind my Maui Jim shades, and felt the stress being sucked out through my pores.

A young woman's voice broke the spell: "Excuse me, sir, may I ask you a question?" She was around 22, blonde, of course, and wore a bikini. None of that was unusual in this neighborhood. Her clipboard was unusual, though, as was the stack of three-by-five papers in her hand.

"I suppose so... Depends on what the question is," I said, feeling a bit hopeful that I was about to enter into a classic middle-aged male fantasy scenario, if you know what I mean.

"I'm doing a study for my business class at USD so I've been polling people here on the beach," she waved her stack of papers.

"And the question is..." I prompted, feeling the fantasy fade.

"What is leadership?" she asked.

A feeling of chilling synchronicity swept over me. I explained to this sun-worshipping surveyor that this was exactly the question I helped people answer every day for a living; that I had worked at one of America's top leadership development firms, The Tom Peters Company, for many years, and that it would take me at least a week and a lot more than a five-inch rectangle of paper to even begin to try to answer that question in a meaningful way. Still, I felt compelled to participate.

I'd heard a wide variety of businesspeople describe leadership; I'd heard consultants describe leadership; and I'd heard the gray-haired pantsuit-and-pumps crowd describe leadership. What I'd never heard was a description from a tongue-pierced, tattooed skater or a bikini-clad rollerblader. Here I was, in the heart of San Diego slacker culture, and suddenly I was dying of curiosity to know what these people on the beach had to say.

"Listen," I said, "I'll make you a deal. I'll write you a definition of leadership straight from the management gurus if you'll show me all of the other responses you've gotten so far."

She readily agreed, so I wrote a line from Jim Kouzes and Barry Posner's book, *The Leadership Challenge*: "Leadership is the art of mobilizing others to want to struggle for shared aspirations." It's a great definition, and Jim is a friend of mine. And besides, it made me feel real smart to be able to manifest a quote out of thin air, as if I was saying *watch this* as I scratched the words down.

Then I collected on my end of the bargain and began to read her little questionnaires. I was shocked; they were right on:

- Gender: female; age: 24; occupation: sales; What is leadership? "Organizing people around a common goal."
- Gender: male; age: 26; occupation: programmer; What is leadership? "Standing up for what you believe in."
- Gender: female; age: 28; occupation: marketing; What is leadership? "Sticking your neck out when it's the right thing to do."

And on it went, just like that. Really good, thoughtful, and, in my opinion, accurate definitions. But then I found the one that said it all.

- Gender: male; age: 23; occupation: unemployed; What is leadership? "If I knew, I'd have a job."

"Now this is brilliant." I said. "'If I knew, I'd have a job.' He's right, I bet."

If even some unemployed slacker sitting on the beach knows how important leadership is, then I'm in the right business, I was thinking as I handed the pile of papers back to her.

"Can I play too?" He had been sitting next to me on the wall, listening to our conversation. "Sure," she said and handed him the clipboard.

"You write it down for me," he said. Salt-and-pepper hair stuck out from under his floppy black beach hat. A newly sprouting goatee pinched up at the corners of his mouth as he smiled. "Four words that describe leadership," he counted them off on his fingers. "Love. Energy. Audacity. Proof."

She wrote on her clipboard.

"That's it?" she asked.

"Yup."

"Want to explain?" she queried, looking a bit befuddled.

"Nah. Shouldn't need to. Except for one thing."

"Yes?"

"That's not just leadership; it's Extreme Leadership."

"Meaning?"

"Think about it for a while. You'll figure it out."

"Oooh... kay..." she said in that exasperated, drawn-out way that suggested eyes rolling behind her shades. She wandered off down the beach.

"That sounded pretty good to me," I said to the dude. *Dude* seemed to be the appropriate label. From his overall getup, the open Hawaiian shirt, Volcom flip-flops slung over his shoulder and baggy khaki shorts, he could have passed for late 20s. But the graying hair and wrinkles around his eyes suggested a few more years. It could have been too much sun. Or too much experience. I couldn't tell.

"It ought to," he said. "I heard you talking. You teach leadership, right?"

"I try to."

"There is no try. Only do," he croaked in a spot-on Yoda voice.

"Oooh... kay..." I said in that drawn-out way that suggested eyes rolling behind my shades. I slid off the wall and stretched, trying to say "Gotta go!" with every bit of body language I could muster.

"Good to meet you..." he extended his hand.

"Steve," I said.

"Edge," he said.

"Come again?"

"Edge. Spelled Edg, with a soft g."

"Edg, as in *on the?*"

"Or *over the.*"

"Okay, Edg, have a good one."

"Always."

Yup. *Dude* was the right label.

■ T W O

Later that night, somewhere between sleeping and dreaming, I kept seeing that goateed face turned up in a smile and hearing his words, "love, energy, audacity, proof," like a persistent mantra. That and the girl's questionnaires got me thinking about my own leadership journey.

As a consultant, I had been a leadership evangelist for many years. I believed that effective leadership could help people to accomplish a couple of significant things at work. First, it would help create a culture so vibrant and healthy that when people woke up in the morning and thought about the imminent workday they wouldn't be overcome with a sense of dread and wouldn't doubt whether or not they could survive the day. Instead, they'd be filled with hope and the knowledge that they could bring themselves fully into their work and do something cool, something significant, something meaningful.

Second, an environment of total engagement would be more likely to create products and services so compelling as to virtually suck clients in the doors.

And even though I still felt as passionate as I ever had, I was beginning to suspect that, perhaps, I was being a touch idealistic. That scared me.

I know a lot of disillusioned consultants. When I was first starting out in my own practice, an older and supposedly wiser man named Patrick, who had built a sterling reputation as an executive coach and corporate change agent, told me that it was impossible to make a difference. No matter what you said or how you said it, no matter if you cajoled or threatened, no matter if you provided overwhelming evidence supporting your clients' need to change, they would never, ever listen to you.

"Then why don't you stop?" I had asked him.

"They pay me too much," was his response.

When the change agent becomes cynical, we're all in deep poop. I chose to dismiss Patrick as an over-the-hill burnout. So I started every project with hope and the conviction that the outcome would rock my client's world. And, with Patrick's sentiment echoing disturbingly in my brain, I ended each project somewhere between feeling mild satisfaction and what I can only describe as, *oh well, maybe next time.*

I was sure, though, that I'd had a positive influence on a good number of people. Right? They always paid me, didn't they? But if all I had done after all these years was broaden a few horizons and help a few folks try something a little different, had I really earned that money? Lying there at 3 a.m., I suspected I had not.

Then why don't I stop? My answer was different from Patrick's, because Patrick was a professional and I am a lunatic. Poet Charles Bukowski said it this way: "The difference between a madman and a professional is that a pro does as well as he can within what he has set out to do and a madman does exceptionally well at what he can't help doing."

I do this work because I can't help it; I have to do it. If that means I'm nuts, so be it.

That was, and I'm not being sarcastic here, a comforting thought that early morning. But love, energy, audacity, and proof? Was that what drove me? That sounded nice; they seemed like noble attributes, but they didn't seem like my attributes. I had to face it, the business of leadership was, for me, just that: a business.

Then it hit me, as the obvious sometimes does when I'm not paying attention, love, energy, audacity, and proof form the acronym LEAP. I'm not normally impressed by acronyms; I am, in fact, a bit leery of them. Many companies try to force fit unpopular, flavor-of-the-month programs into snappy, acronymic labels like QUALCRAP: quality circles, results, accountability, progress.

But the fact that LEAP was an acronym raised some interesting questions about Edg. Where did LEAP come from? Did Edg hear it somewhere or was it his own insight and creation? Was he talking from experience or just talking?

Alone in my room in peaceful predawn San Diego, I found myself curiouser and curiouser about the dude called Edg.

Curiosity killed the cat, the saying goes, and satisfaction brought him back.

Wednesday

■ THREE

The next morning, I walked out to the boardwalk sipping a triple shot mocha and hoping that the caffeine would kick in quickly after my restless night. I walked down to the water, stuck my toes in, and watched the surfers zipping along the waves. They'd been out there since dawn, I was sure, just as they were every morning. They had the surf; I had caffeine.

"You surf?"

I jumped, splashing my morning fix into the sand. It was Edg, standing right behind me and leaning on his board, obviously delighted that he'd startled the foam out of me.

"No. I like to watch."

"Don't know what you're missing."

"Yes, I do. About three sips of precious fluids."

The water rushed in and cleaned up around my feet.

"Sorry about that," he said, not meaning a word. "Let me make it up to you. You can buy us both another cup."

I followed him up the sand toward the boardwalk, thinking that at the very least, it could be fun to spend a little time with a fellow smart-ass. We walked up the stairs to Canes Rooftop Grill. Edg leaned his surfboard against the wall and pulled a couple of stools up to the ledge overlooking the ocean.

As the waitress poured our coffee, I was plotting to satisfy my curiosity about Edg by digging around with inconspicuous small talk. I'd ask him where, if at all, he was working, where he lived, all the usual first conversation stuff. But I never got the chance.

"Watch that surfer," said Edg, pointing out over the water. I watched the guy paddle his board in toward the shore and stand up as the wave started to break. He rode for a very short time before falling ass-over-teakettle into the water as the wave crashed onto his head.

"Ouch!" I said.

"Wrong response, man. That's what the sport is about. What you just saw there was a victory."

"And the ocean won," I said.

"No. It's not that kind of victory. There's no winner and loser in this; it's not a zero-sum game. If you have to think of it that way, the surfer won some great experience that'll help him ride bigger waves later on. That's why every wipeout is a victory for the surfer. Same is true in your line of work."

"I feel a metaphor coming on," I said, finishing my coffee.

"Right. You got a problem with metaphors?"

"*Au contraire.* But spell it out for me."

"Surfing is an extreme sport because the wipeout is part of it. All extreme sports have that in common. And leadership, metaphorically speaking, is an extreme sport, too."

"You've got to be willing to take a risk. There's nothing new in that." I made a futile attempt to flag down our waitress.

"Very easy to say, but in business, especially, very hard to do. The irony is risk is a natural part of the human experience, and we accept it in many areas of our lives without realizing it. But a lot of businesspeople who call themselves leaders want things to be easy and painless. They're either kidding themselves or lying."

"Strong words."

"Look how people are dressed," he said, sweeping his hand over the boardwalk below. "Do you have kids?"

"Yeah."

"Do they wear baggy pants like those?"

"Oh, yeah."

"Do they skate?"

"A little."

"Skateboarders developed that style so they could wear kneepads under their clothes. But most people who wear baggy clothes have never even touched a skateboard. They're called *posers*; they want you to think they're risk takers, and real skaters can't stand them. Posers try to grab the skaters' glory without putting themselves at risk. But wearing the pants doesn't make you a skater, wearing spandex doesn't make you a cyclist, looking at the world through

Oakley shades doesn't make you a snowboarder, saying 'dude' doesn't make you a surfer and, in business, printing 'leader' on your calling card doesn't mean squat. People who wear 'leader' as a label without putting themselves wholeheartedly into the act of leading are just like fashion hounds; they're the posers of the business world."

The color was rising in Edg's already sun-reddened face. He still had a little half smile, but I could tell he didn't really find this funny at all.

"So they talk but don't walk," I said. "Kind of like the people that use all the new management buzzwords and leave it at that." That really got him going.

"It's a con job, is what it is," he said, his voice getting a little too loud for a public place. "These posers latch on to new jargon and catchphrases, but they don't do anything different. You ever been *empowered*, Steve? You ever *empower* anybody?"

"I suppose so, yeah. But that's hardly a new buzzword."

"No, it's not new, but let me show you what it typically looks like. Let's say you work for me." He pushed his stool back from the ledge and stood over me. "My boss recently came back from an off-site where they talked about empowerment, and she's got the religion now. So, the first thing she does back in the office is fire off an email to all of her direct reports, including me, saying that from now on we're going to *empower* people around here. So, now I'm going to *empower* you. What's my motivation here? Why am I going to do this?"

"Your boss told you to."

"Exactly. I damn well better or I may get reengineered out of a job."

He began his little demonstration.

"What does empowerment mean to you, Steve?"

"Well, it's..."

"I'll tell you what it means. It means that from now on *you* are gonna start making decisions to take better care of our customers and improve our processes and all that garbage. Got it?"

"Yessir," I said, being the good little role-player.

He raised his arms and waggled his fingers over my head.

"Feel anything?"

"Yessir," I said, still playing along.

"You better," he said, waggling enthusiastically. "Steve, I empower you to go out there and make decisions to please the customer, yada, yada, yada. Now go forth and be thou empowered. A little advice, however: DON'T SCREW IT UP. And before you make any decisions, check with me."

I chuckled as he received a round of applause from the folks at the next table.

"Okay, I get it," I said. "That's a poser talking."

"Exactly," he said, perching back on his barstool. "That's using a new buzzword with the same old garbage associated with it, behaviorally speaking. It's not empowerment."

We talked about all the buzzwords we'd heard over the years. It was like visiting the Management Jargon Hall of

Fame, including such classics as MBO, MBWA, customer focus, quality circles, learning organization, value-add, thinking outside the box, excellence, downsizing, rightsizing, flattening, densepacking—don't ask me what *that* means—and reengineering to name, believe it or not, a few.

I remembered when Michael Hammer and James Champy's *Reengineering the Corporation* came out in paperback in May of 1994, how businesspeople stopped "changing" things and started "reengineering" them—move your stapler from the left side of your desk to the right side and *voilà!* you've reengineered your workspace. I had a friend going through a divorce at the time who told me he was "reengineering his domestic strategy." Very few people and organizations really understood the meaning and methodology that Hammer and Champy intended, and consequently didn't really reengineer anything, but they sure knew how to use the word in a sentence. This later led Champy to another conclusion: "If management doesn't change, reengineering will be stopped in its tracks."

Leadership, we agreed, was another one of those buzzwords. "Everybody calls himself or herself a leader nowadays," said Edg. "We used to go to management training, and now we go to leadership training. We are team leaders, program leaders, project leaders, thought leaders, market leaders, and cheerleaders. We are political leaders, and we are community leaders. We lead our companies, we lead our families, and we lead our lives. We have diluted the meaning of leadership to such a profound degree that it's become just another label. But leadership is not that easy, so we con ourselves into believing that the word is the same as the action."

"'Con' is a bit hyperbolic, don't you think?"

"Isn't that what a con artist does?" he asked. "He'll promise a sure thing. He'll offer you ease and security without any possible chance of falling or failing. He'll guarantee what you want, when you want it. Then he'll take your life's savings, scoot off to the Caymans, and suck piña coladas squeezed from your hard-earned pineapples. We are our own worst con artists if we use safety and security in the same sentence as leadership.

"The ability to lead doesn't come from a snappy vocabulary, the books you've displayed on your shelves, your place on the organizational chart or that fashionable title on your business card. Leadership is always substantive and rarely fashionable. It is intensely personal and intrinsically scary, and it requires us to live the ideas we espouse, in irrefutable ways, every day of our lives, up to and beyond the point of fear."

"So, we're back to leadership as an extreme sport," I said, trying to pull a thread through the rant.

"Yeah. Extreme Leadership is what I'm talking about. Living in pursuit of the OSM."

■ FOUR

By this time, it was clear to me that Edg was no beach bum. At least not full time. He had obviously been around the corporate world in some capacity, and his conclusions were very similar to my own, which in and of itself didn't lend him any credibility. But I still didn't know a thing about him. Once again, I was going to ask him for his credentials, as it were, and I was going to ask how he'd come up with that LEAP idea, but he distracted me with another damn acronym.

"What, dare I ask, is an OSM?"

Edg called the waitress over and asked for more coffee and a pen. "First, you have to learn how to spell it." He grabbed a napkin and scribbled. "Like this: capital O, capital S, exclamation point, capital M. OS!M." He stirred his coffee with the pen.

"And that stands for...?"

"I'll give you an example. Then you tell me what it stands for."

"Okay," I agreed, without his asking me to.

"You know what street luge is?"

"Like regular luge without the snow?"

"Close enough. Now, imagine that you're lying flat on your back on a long, wheeled sled, kinda like a skateboard, perched on the top of a steep hill. This isn't your serene, pastoral, snow-covered hill; it's an asphalt slope lined on both sides by parked cars. At the bottom of the hill, a quarter of a mile away, is a major intersection. And the traffic light down there is your finish line. Get the picture?

"Your friend pats you on the helmet, gives you a mighty thrust toward Main Street, and whoosh! You are gravity's love slave. The asphalt is blazing two inches under your back, parked cars are screaming past your head, and you can't stop, you can't turn back, and right there, in that moment, there are only two words on your mind. What are they?"

"Oh Shit!" I yelled, momentarily stopping the conversation around us.

"Exactamundo!" exclaimed Edg. "Now, picture this: You'd been preparing to give a presentation to the executive team of an important prospective client. You and your team had worked for days on the numbers, the graphics, and the perfect words. You had practiced in front of the mirror until it cracked, you had mumbled the entire spiel in your sleep for a week–so says your spouse–and now you're walking across plush gray carpet to the front of the boardroom. You reach the oak podium, turn, and look out at the grim audience of folded arms and Brooks Brothers suits, and you can't run away. Right there, in that moment, what are you thinking?"

"I want my mommy?"

"Try to stay with the theme here, Stevie."

"Okay. Oh Shit! Again."

"Right! OS!M. You've just had an Oh Shit! Moment, and it's the natural, built-in human indicator that you are doing, or are about to do, something truly significant and you are, rightfully, scared out of your gourd."

"And you're saying that's a good thing?"

"Absolutely. We've been conditioned to believe that fear is bad. And, yeah, fear can save your life or keep you from doing something stupid, but avoiding it can also keep you from doing something great, from learning something new, and from growing as a human being. Fear is a natural part of growth, and since growth, change, and evolution are all on the Extreme Leader's agenda, fear comes with the territory."

"So, the Extreme Leader pursues the OS!M."

"Yeah, but that's the easy part. Pursuing the OS!M, as I just described it, is a private, personal endeavor. But a leader lives under a microscope. I'm not saying it's fair or just, but people watch everything the leader does. Everything. They watch the body language and facial expressions, they listen to the tone of voice, they observe the decisions the leader makes, they listen to the leader's questions and how they're asked. Therefore, the most powerful tool a leader has is himself or herself."

"Leading by example. What does that have to do with the OS!M?"

"Simple. When you have your OS!Ms publicly, for everyone to see, you send a message that says we should all be doing this. This idea scares the hell out of most businesspeople. But I'll tell you, man, there are people in this world who love to screw up in public. It's their way of proving the power of their own convictions."

I was skeptical. While every business book I'd ever picked up talked about how important it was to encourage people to take risks and learn from their mistakes, I hadn't met many managers who relished the experience of falling on their own face. "Like who?" I asked.

"Like this rock climber from Adelaide, Australia. He was freestyling, that means no ropes and no harnesses, with a partner. He tried a new move, stretched just a little too far for his next handhold, and fell 11 meters off the mountain and landed in an olive tree. As he came to in the tree, he pulled an olive branch out of his side and realized that he was lucky to be alive. He looked up at his horrified climbing partner still clinging to the mountain and called out to him. Now ask yourself. If that were you impaled on that tree, what would you yell to your buddy?"

"Get help!" I said.

"Most people would. Here's what he said: 'Did you get that on film?'

"The only thing on that climber's mind in that near-death moment was the thrill he would get in sharing his muff with his mates. He wanted them to see that he was gutsy enough to attempt the audacious, even if he failed trying. That scar in his gut was his lesion of honor. That's not how most businesspeople operate, is it? Is that how you approach your work, Steve?"

"Meaning what?" I asked, wondering how I had suddenly become the subject of the conversation.

"Meaning this: You're leading an important project at work; you try something new, and it bombs. Miserably.

You've skewered yourself in the olive tree. Do you yell, 'Hey! Everybody see how I screwed up there? Did we get that on film?' Probably not. The only reason you may want that film is to destroy the evidence, not to share it."

"I get the point, but I'm not so sure how comfortable I'd be having my failures immortalized."

"Comfortable!" he snorted. "Whoever said leadership is comfortable? You're missing the whole freakin' point: You screw up every day, and *everyone already knows it*. But when you show us that you can face your own screw-ups, when you can publicly acknowledge that you crashed and burned, when you can, metaphorically speaking, hoist your shirt in front of a hundred people to show us the scar that you earned when you fell off the mountain, we'll be closer to you as human beings. And we follow human beings; we don't follow idealized icons of unattainable perfection."

I knew he was right. And an image of me as a kid rushed into my head: I devoured Superman comics by the pound and thumbed them until my fingers were inked up and my imagination was soaring. The Man of Steel was cool because of his superpowers: he had X-ray vision, he could fly, he could handle any adversary. But ultimately, it was his imperfection that made him believable and compelling. He hid behind Clark Kent, his heart was torn between Lois and Lana, he grieved for his real parents and loved his foster ones, and he lived in constant fear of kryptonite. If the Invulnerable Man really were invulnerable, I'd have directed my loyalties to Disney comics.

Too many businesspeople, myself included, as Edg had pointed out, wanted to be invincible. They confused credibility with perfection and, therefore, would never dream of showing their scars and foibles to their employees. Asking them to have their OS!Ms in public would be like asking them to chew glass. I could think of one leader, though, who did pursue his own OS!Ms with the full participation of his team, and I shared the story with Edg.

■ FIVE

As a regional manager at a major brokerage firm, Michael had been working on his own leadership skills for several years. Despite his efforts, however, his retail branch region had consistently ranked last or second to last in his company's employee opinion survey. And in this rare company where surveys were taken seriously—the results were published and ranked—this was bad news for Michael's career. He was losing his credibility as a manager. Then he had an epiphany.

Even though the surveys specifically reflected the views of frontline branch employees whose lives were affected by their immediate supervisors, Michael assumed he was the problem, not the supervisors.

So he gathered his management team together, stood up in front of the conference room, and said: "I'm screwing up, and the numbers show it, so I want you to tell me what

I'm doing wrong and what I need to do to improve." That was OS!M number one, I figured.

"I'm going to leave the room," he went on, "and I'd like you to get very specific and write down your ideas on flip-chart paper. When I come back, we'll talk through each item."

And he walked out. OS!M number two.

A half-hour later, he came back and knocked on the door. "We're not done yet," they said. Major OS!M.

Finally, after 90 minutes, they let him in. The walls were covered in flip-chart paper with list after list of, what shall we call them, suggestions for his personal improvement as a human being. Monumental OS!M.

Michael knew that his reaction in that moment would make or break the whole exercise, as well as his personal credibility. So he took a radical approach and responded authentically.

"I'm really disappointed," he said, "in myself. I had no idea there'd be so much."

He didn't defend, justify, or make excuses. All he did was ask some questions to make sure he fully understood each item, and they talked together for the next couple of hours.

That night and the next couple of days, Michael told me, were the most difficult of his entire career. He was devastated and overwhelmed by the severity of the feedback and the immense challenge to follow through. He recovered from the initial shock, however, and the next round of surveys ranked Michael's organization second from the top in the entire company, with jumps of 80 to 90% in some measures. That's a leap no matter how you look at it. But the funny thing is, the improvement had relatively little to do with Michael's follow-up actions. It had everything to do with his team.

Without his asking them to, Michael's managers, inspired by the experience, went back to their branches and did the same thing with their folks. And for the first time, employees were personally engaged in the improvement of their own work environment.

By publicly seeking out those OS!Ms, Michael not only jump-started his organization, he also blasted his own career into orbit. As his reputation as a leader spread, he was promoted, with the near-unanimous recommendation of his direct reports, to take responsibility for the entire U.S. branch office operations.

"Great example," said Edg. "Michael willingly scared the hell out of himself, because he knew that getting intensely personal feedback would be the only way to improve things. And that ultimately led to his and his team's success and to the heart of the matter: When necessary, the Extreme Leader will risk his or her own safety and security in order to grow the business and, just as importantly, develop as a human being.

"Safety isn't bad, but we often arrive at it by way of hazard and by learning from every break, scrape, and bruise. It often comes through the knowledge gained by having been unsafe. But the OS!M isn't about taking stupid risks, and it's not about putting yourself in harm's way for the hell of it or for some kind of gratuitous adrenaline rush. It's not about nauseating yourself or making yourself sick, though you may get sick in the process.

"You've heard of Jimmy Shea, the gold medalist for men's skeleton from the 2002 Winter Olympics?"

"Yeah. I saw him win it. That's some crazy stuff, those guys screaming down the track head first with their chins a few inches off the ground."

"Radical, huh?" he said with obvious delight. "An interviewer asked Shea if he could recall his first time doing skeleton, and he said, 'Oh, yeah. I felt like I'd just made the biggest mistake of my life. But when I got to the bottom, I couldn't wait to get back up and do it again.' No OS!M, no gold medal."

"So the OS!M in the right context is an indicator of growth," I summarized.

"Think of it like this: If the only reason you're avoiding taking on a challenge is because the idea scares you, then *that's the reason to take it on.* You have to pursue the OS!M, dude. That's how you know you're growing as a leader. And the bigger and more important the challenge, the more intense the OS!M."

"So the Extreme Leader takes on extreme challenges?"

He glanced at his watch. "Tell me what you think of this. Carly Fiorina, as controversial as she was as the CEO of Hewlett-Packard, nailed it when she told an MIT graduating class that 'a leader's greatest obligation is to make possible an environment where people can aspire to change the world.' Is that extreme enough for you?"

I had also read Carly's speech—apparently Edg and I had some common source—but now I thought about it in terms of the OS!M. "Changing the world. Yeah, I'd say that qualifies."

"Let me put it bluntly," said Edg, as he stood and scooped his surfboard under his arm. "If you're using all the buzzwords, reading all the latest books, and holding forth at every meeting on the latest management fads, but you're *not* experiencing that visceral churning in your gut, *not* scaring yourself every day, *not* feeling that Oh Shit! Moment like clockwork, then you're *not* doing anything significant, let alone changing the world. And you're *certainly not leading anyone else.* But you'll sure look snappy in your big, baggy pants."

He tapped a finger on the check, pointed at me, gave me a stiff salute, and turned to walk away. I waved good-bye to the back of his head and looked out over the ocean just as another surfer kissed the brine.

Thursday

■ S I X

Intuition: it's the way a grandfather clock sounds at one second before midnight, or the way the phone sounds just before it rings. Phones don't actually ring anymore; they chirp, burble, vibrate; they chime a little tune like "Sailor's Hornpipe" or the theme to the Muppet Show. My kitchen phone burbled at the same moment as my oatmeal. I turned off the range and reached for the handset, with the gnawing feeling that this call would be important.

I had spent another restless night with Edg, not literally, you understand, thinking about our conversation at Canes, and it became blazingly clear to me that my life had been a series of leaps from one OS!M to another.

When I was 17, I graduated high school a semester early, moved from suburban Chicago to New York City— over my father's impassioned protests—and lived in a tenement apartment with my friend Sam and a couple of other free-spirited (meaning, unemployed) guys. Believe me, every day is jammed with OS!Ms when you're trying to survive on toast and Nestlé's Quik. But I grew up fast, and

I wouldn't trade a nanosecond of my experience during that time.

By the time I was 29, I had lived in Israel for a year, started a folk/bluegrass band, terminated the folk/bluegrass band, started college, graduated college, started a rock band, gotten married, terminated the rock band, had three children, and started my own small brokerage firm.

My business had been a relentless struggle from day one: cash flow problems at work and at home, deception from people that I had viewed as trusted friends and advisors, and, finally, a partner who had bailed out on me at the worst possible moment. The last words I ever heard him say were, "I'm sending you a wire for $25,000." The wire never came, I closed up shop, and he and I never spoke to or saw each other again. I wiped out, went down in a blaze of glory, crashed and burned, pick your metaphor, but I had learned how to, and more importantly, how not to, run a business. It turned out to be a great, invaluable, fabulous lesson that ultimately led me into my present career, but at the time, it didn't put oatmeal on the kiddies' breakfast table. Then I turned 30.

That felt like a lifetime ago. And it felt like a minute. OS!M, OS!M, OS!M.

"Yellow!" I said into the phone.

"Steve?"

"That's me," I confirmed.

"It's Janice."

"Janice! Man, oh man, I haven't talked to you in..."

"I think I'm about to get fired."

Janice had started out several years ago as my client and, during the course of a long consulting project, had become my friend. She was a dynamo who was accused of being a bit too aggressive at times except, of course, when she brought home the results. But she had a perpetual, infectious, and completely genuine smile that drew people to her, and an open heart that kept them there.

She was one of the few executives I'd met who really took personal development, hers and others', seriously. And believe me, I've met many executives over the years who gave up on their own leadership initiatives as soon as it became inconvenient or the organizational chart above them changed.

I remember a senior VP named Ron, a self-proclaimed cynic about *corporate change initiatives*, who experienced a sudden conversion to being a great champion of the company's new customer service training. One day he hated the whole damned thing and talked it down every chance he got; the next day he was standing on his soapbox in front of union employees and waxing eloquent on how marvelous this program was going to be.

A changed man? Hardly. The company had reorganized and Ron had suddenly found himself reporting to the program's sponsor.

"I took one look at the new org chart," said Ron, "and I realized how much I *love* this thing."

Janice was not like that. She had an internal sense of right and wrong and challenged herself to live up to it whether or not the environment around her supported it.

She had a center of gravity, while people like Ron tumbled through space, hoping to find orbit around someone else's point of view.

Now, apparently, she was in trouble. I wasn't surprised, though. Her company, a biotech firm called XinoniX, had recently brought in a new CEO, and the president had subsequently left under the pretense of early retirement. Rumors were flying about what had really happened, with some folks speculating that Teddy Garrison, president and founder, had locked horns with the new guy and decided to bail. Garrison had hired Janice and made her senior vice president of marketing and his *de facto* second-in-command. They had been together since the first day XinoniX opened its doors.

"I really wanted to make it work, even though Garrison was gone," said Janice. "He left a great legacy and culture here. We were doing some very cool things right at the forefront of genetic modeling, and everybody was jazzed. Before he left, Teddy handed me the torch. I mean, he *literally* handed me a tiki torch and told me that it was up to me to keep things going, to keep the place lively, fun, and fast. To keep it XinoniX, in other words."

"And?" I prompted.

"And he left. Just like that. That was a month ago, and nobody's heard from him. I don't have any idea where he is, and I feel like I've been left out here to dry up and blow away. I can't believe he would just walk away from us. XinoniX was Teddy's baby, and I don't think it's an exaggeration to say that every employee from top to bottom would have followed him anywhere. This was our baby, too."

"But you stayed."

"Yeah, I stayed. I put the torch in my office as a reminder and went to battle with the new guy."

"What's his story?" I asked, knowing that there had to be one.

"I think this sums it up: His nickname at his previous company was The 51% Guy."

I hadn't really been following the XinoniX story in the business press, so I hadn't heard the new CEO's name, but hearing that handle gave me chills. I told Janice that I knew The 51% Guy; he had hired me several years ago at his company to "teach leadership to those people." He hadn't said it that way, exactly, but as it turned out, that was the gist of it. He was infamous among the employee ranks for two incidents that epitomized his management approach.

Once, at an all hands meeting, he had stood up and said: "I want your input and opinions on things around here. I want to know what you think. Just remember, I have 51% of the vote." The employees had been so angry that they were still telling the story ten years later when I showed up. The 51% rule, as it came to be known, meant, "Talk all you want, but this is my show. If you don't like it, go home." And judging by his nickname, it was his legacy. When I first heard that story from some employees in the company's distribution center, I wondered if he'd been misunderstood. Maybe, I had said to them, he was trying to say that he wanted their ideas, and that he'd use that valuable input in making his decisions which, I added, is a very smart way to run a business. They laughed at me.

Around the same time of his little speech, apparently, a few of the employees were in his office offering their valuable insights into the improvement of the distribution center, and in the middle of the conversation, The 51% Guy picked up a glass of water from his desk and said: "You see the water level in this glass? Watch what happens when I stick my finger in there. See how the level doesn't change much if my finger is in the water or out? See that?" He wagged his moist index finger in front of their faces. "This is you," he said. "Whether you're here, *dunk*, or not, *wag*, makes no difference to us."

I knew this wasn't hard science, but when I put the 51% speech together with the finger-dipping analogy, I got pretty clear anecdotal evidence that The 51% Guy was an autocrat at best, and more likely a dictator. The leadership training that he'd sponsored was nothing more than a vain attempt to bolster his image. The 51% Guy, Bob Jeffers was his name, was a poser.

"That's him," said Janice. "It was clear from the start that he's the only one on his agenda."

"So you and Jeffers don't see eye to eye, I'm guessing."

"First he tolerated me, then he fought me on everything, and now he's ignoring me. In other words..."

"You think you're about to get canned?"

"Yeah, if I don't quit first. And I need your help."

I was already thinking about companies I knew that would snap Janice up in a heartbeat, but I was confused about why she was coming to me. She knew everybody in the San Diego business community and had a great reputation in her field.

"I need to find Garrison."

"I don't understand," I said.

"What I mean is I want you to help me find him."

"Me? Who am I? Sam Spade?"

"Listen, Steve," she said. "I told him about the work you did with me, and he said that he really wanted to meet you. I think if you could find him, he'd talk to you."

"And then what?"

"You can talk him into coming back."

"So... you really want to stay at XinoniX?"

"Only if things change."

"Okay. I'll see what I can do, but only on one condition."

"I'm listening."

"You don't quit. And you and I start working on what you're going to do at XinoniX if Garrison's answer is no."

She hesitated on the no-quit clause and then said, "Deal."

So, I promised Janice that I'd call around. I did have a little time before my next trip, and, who knows, this could be kind of fun. *I'm going to need a new notebook,* I thought to myself in a voice vaguely reminiscent of Humphrey Bogart, *and a trench coat.*

"What makes Garrison so special?" I asked before I signed off.

"Well, there are a lot of specifics. He's smart, charming, a great visionary, and all that, but there's one thing about him that stands out above everything else."

"What's that?"

"He loved this place."

■ SEVEN

Apparently, it had happened this way: Janice had gone to work that morning after our chat and conducted her traditional morning rounds of cubicle city. She always made a point of checking in with everyone on her staff before the chaos of the day came crashing down, and lately she'd been particularly vigilant. Her team had been busting its hump to finish its new marketing plan, and they were more exhausted than usual. The morning's informal face-to-face with their ostensibly fearless leader meant a great deal to the team, Janice knew, but it also gave her the emotional boost she needed to get through another day in the new XinoniX regime.

This day seemed to promise no more turbulence than usual. That is, until she found the Post-it note on her computer screen. It said: "My office. Now. Jeffers."

She peeled the note off the screen and, with her blood pressure on the rise, headed off down the hall.

This, apparently, is how it happened: Her new boss invited Janice into his office and asked her to have a seat in the plush, leather banker's chair. He sat behind his desk, perched on his wingback, ergonomically designed Herman Miller marvel, several inches above Janice's line of sight. He held up the lime green folder that contained Janice's team's marketing plan, ceremoniously waved it in front of his face, swiveled his chair efficiently to the right, and dumped the contents into the trash can.

And then, apparently, without a word, without a whisper, without so much as a grunt or a sigh, Robert J. Jeffers, The 51% Guy, got up and left Janice alone in his office.

■ EIGHT

I was back at Canes enjoying an afternoon shot of espresso and thinking about my new role as the accidental sleuth. The connection, such as it was, with Janice, Jeffers, and me was too eerie to ignore. Synchronicity is what they call it, I think; I call it eerie. Still, I had no idea where to start looking for Garrison; I was having a hard enough time finding myself, let alone anyone else.

"Dude!" He had a way of sneaking up on me.

"Were you looking for me," I asked, "or is this just a happy coincidence?"

"I think it's called synchronicity," he said, sending a ripple up my spine. He was wearing a bright yellow Hawaiian shirt patterned with ripe, bulbous pineapples. I could see his eyes crinkling into a smile behind small, round sunglasses. He was, once again, the picture of beach hip.

"I've been thinking about you," said Edg as he parked himself at my table. "You and I have a lot to talk about, so I want you to meet me every day for the next four days."

"And I want *you* to dance the hula with a bone in your nose," I said.

"Really?" He seemed to be considering the possibility. "Why?"

"I guess I'm asking you the same question, Edg."

"At the risk of sounding mysterious," he said, "I'll just say that we'd be doing each other a great favor."

Well, that did sound mysterious and, frankly, a little bit wacky. I guess that's why I agreed. Besides, the truth was that I'd been thinking about him, too, and I had a few questions that lingered from the day before. I explained to him that I was working on a project for a friend and wasn't sure how much of my time that would chew up, so he'd have to be flexible with the schedule. "And what, exactly, is on the agenda for our daily meetings?" I asked.

"LEAP," said Edg.

And we did. Right into my car.

■ N I N E

"Where are we going?" I asked, feeling odd because I was the one driving.

"Go north, young man," said my passenger as he stuck his head, doglike, out the side of my Mustang convertible.

We drove in silence up the coast toward North County, San Diego. We passed through Pacific Beach, La Jolla, and

Del Mar, places known throughout the world for their beauty and wealth. Prime real estate with ocean views. You can get yourself a nice little pad for a few mil. I made a mental note to do that as soon as possible.

As we passed through Solana Beach, Edg directed me to turn right into a boulder-bordered driveway. I swung the Mustang eastward. The ocean view disappeared and, suddenly and shockingly, we were driving through a trailer park. A trailer park? Along the ocean? I didn't know which was stranger, the fact that it was here at all or that I'd never noticed it before.

"This where you live?" I asked.

He pointed ahead up the narrow, shrub-lined street. "Park there," he ordered, obviously ignoring my question.

"Ain't you the cryptic one," I said as I pulled the car over.

"Let's go!" He launched himself over the car door and ran up the pathway to a doublewide with a red rose bush planted on either side of the faux oak door and, without knocking, disappeared inside.

"Okay... I just need to turn the car off and close the top and stuff like that," I muttered to myself, "and I'll be right along. Go right ahead; don't wait for me..."

He'd left the trailer's door open, so I took that as an invitation and stepped over the threshold as fragrant rose-scented air filled my head.

I've always expected trailers to be dark and uninviting, but this one was filled with sunlight from a floor-to-ceiling bay window that looked out over a small, meticulous garden of bougainvillea, jasmine, and more red roses. Edg was standing out there with an older man, and they were just dropping their arms from what had obviously been a very warm embrace. They both looked my way and gestured for me to join them.

As I passed through the French doors, the man grasped my right hand firmly in his own and put his left hand on my elbow. His short, silver hair, glistening in the sunlight, was dramatically set off against his dark brown skin. He was a blend of African and Asian descent, I thought, and he reminded me of people I'd met in Trinidad several years before, who were some of the most exotically beautiful people I'd ever seen.

I know that it's a cliché to describe someone's eyes as twinkling or bright as if lit from within, but you'll have to excuse me because they were. And the relative darkness of his skin made his gray-blue sparklies even more noticeable as they locked onto me. His smile was full and warm and somehow familiar.

"Steve, meet Pops. Pops, Steve," said Edg.

"All my friends call me Pops," Pops reassured. "And I'd consider it an honor if you would, too."

He could have finished his sentence with, *this is CNN*, and I wouldn't have been surprised. His voice was as deep and resonant as James Earl Jones's.

We sat down at a small table under a jasmine-laced lattice, and Pops poured the three of us water with slices of lemon and orange floating on the top from a wide pitcher.

"I've told Pops all about you," Edg said with a bit of mischief in his voice, "and I think you already know a lot about him."

"Sorry, I don't..."

"William G. Maritime is what I'm called by the world at large," said Pops, also with a bit of mischief in his voice, "especially by the business press."

I must have looked really brilliant with my mouth hanging open like that. William Maritime was a veritable business god. He was kind of a cross between a less flamboyant Richard Branson and a less explosive Ted Turner with a dash of Mother Teresa thrown in for depth. No wonder his smile was familiar, I'd seen it on the cover of *Forbes* and *Businessweek* as well as *People* and—I wasn't sure about this one—the *National Enquirer*. I seemed to remember a headline that said something like "Mystery Multimillionaire Maritime Marries Martian in Secret Ceremony." But I might have made that up.

What I did know was W. G. Maritime and Son was one big-ass company with a reputation for both bottom-line performance and community responsibility. It was one of those enlightened companies that management gurus were always talking about, and it was frequently cited as one of the top ten companies to work for in America. William Maritime's quotes were almost as ubiquitous as Jack Welch's. I myself had a PowerPoint slide saying,

> "Love the players or lose the game."
> —William Maritime
> CEO, W.G. Maritime and Son

I wasn't entirely sure what it meant.

He had started out in the boat leasing business and over time had diversified, GE-like, into everything from entertainment to industrial steam cleaning equipment. And then, one day a number of years ago, he retired and all but vanished from the public eye. That was a fact, but whether or not he retired to marry a Martian was, to my knowledge, never verified. What was irrefutable, though, was that the man was a legend, and the legend had just poured me a glass of water in a small garden behind his trailer home.

"I...," I said confidently, "I... am," I continued, building on my original proposition, "in the Twilight Zone, right?"

Edg howled, clearly delighted by watching me scramble for equilibrium. "No, it's the real world, dude. Trust me on that."

"Edg and I go back a ways," said William 'Pops' Maritime, "and when he told me about your chance meeting and subsequent conversation, I asked him to bring you along on his next visit. So here we are. Good enough?"

"Sure," I said. "But we gotta make it snappy, because I'm expected for high tea at Buckingham Palace."

"Good sign," said Pops, grinning in the sharp sunlight. "The shock passes quickly."

■ T E N

If you had told me this morning that by midday I'd be sipping citrus water with William Maritime, I'd have laughed in your face. But there, undeniably, I was, and I wasn't going to miss this opportunity to pick his very large, iconoclastic brain.

"Have you heard of the term 'OS!M'?" I asked, testing to see if he and Edg had ever had that conversation.

"I sure have," he said.

"What do you have to say on the subject?"

"The boy got your attention, didn't he?" said Pops, cocking his thumb toward Edg. "Well, it's a clever acronym, and it's memorable as a concept, and there's certainly no doubt that it's a legitimate and important aspect of the human experience in general and the leadership experience in particular." He paused and took a long, thoughtful sip of water. "But if you stop there, you miss the whole point of leadership."

"Which is what?" When that question leapt, reflexively, from my lips, I felt immediately childish. He must have meant that in a rhetorical way. Leadership is a multifaceted, complex subject; it can't have a whole point. I was being naïve to think that he was actually intending to complete the thought. But my question hung there in the air like a small but conspicuous cloud of cigarette smoke, too late to be sucked back in unnoticed.

He looked at me, expressionless.

"Never mind. Stupid question," I backpedaled. "There's no such thing."

"Let me ask you a 'stupid question,' Mr. Farber. Why do you care?"

"Well, assuming that there actually is a whole point of leadership, I care because I'm a student of the subject. I care because it's my job to help businesspeople to be better leaders, and I care because..." I heard my own voice trailing off and echoing down a long, empty cavern to nowhere.

"So the answer is 'because,'" he said.

"I know I can do better than that. You just caught me off guard."

He let me off the hook with a wide, warm grin. "I understand. Very few businesspeople take the time to reflect on why they care about anything they do: why they care about the decisions they make, why they care about their customers and employees, or why they care about their business beyond the paycheck. So don't feel bad. But that's one question that will never catch a true leader *off guard*, as you say."

"But aren't you making a rather big assumption there?"

"Am I?"

"I think so. In order for business leaders to know *why* they care, you're assuming that they do. Care, that is."

"Of course."

"Are you telling me that managers, supervisors, and executives are always motivated by caring?"

"Of course not."

"I didn't think so."

"Leaders are."

"Actually," Edg jumped in, "care doesn't even touch it, does it, Pops?"

"No, it doesn't. I use the word *care* just to get us started. Care is a somewhat politically correct, watered-down version of the leader's true motivation. For an Extreme Leader, as Edg likes to say, it goes much, much deeper."

"So, Extreme Leaders are not motivated by caring?" I asked.

"Don't overcomplicate it, son. Of course they care, but their caring is rooted, ultimately, in love."

"Love." I repeated, with a splash of skepticism in my vocal tonic. I sat for a moment and let the idea sink in. "Love of what?"

"Exactly. Love of what. Love of what future we're trying to create together," Pops said, switching suddenly to the first person point of view. "Love of what principle we're trying to live out, love of what people I have around me, and love of what they want for their lives. Love of what customers I have, and love of what customers I might have in the future if I'm smarter, faster, and more creative in serving their needs. Love of what impact we can have on the lives of our customers and, if we're audacious enough, on the world as a whole. Love of what our business really is, and love for what, when we cut away the chaff, we really do at work every day."

He paused for a moment, as if to gather his thoughts, although they didn't seem to need any gathering. They were coming at me in laser-like, fully coherent force and concentration. Maybe the pause was for my benefit.

"If I love who we are, and if I love what we can be, then I'll love the process of how we get there. And in order to make it all happen, I will act boldly and courageously and I will, at times, fail magnificently. But my love demands that I try. *Demands* it."

"'A pro does as well as he can within what he has set out to do, and a madman does exceptionally well at what he can't help doing,'" I said.

"Bukowski!" Pops and Edg exclaimed simultaneously.

"Jinx!" cried Edg, which had the charming and curious effect of cracking them both up.

"Bukowski, despite his drunken philandering," Pops continued, dabbing at his laughter-teared eyes, "got that one exactly right. It's the madness of love that I'm talking about. Or, at least it can look like madness to those who don't share the same passion.

"The title of that Bukowski poem is also apropos here: 'What Matters Most Is How Well You Walk through the Fire.' In the context of our conversation, having love and doing nothing about it isn't leadership by anyone's definition. You have to express it. You have to walk through the fire. And in trying to express my love in real, tangible, and meaningful ways, I will experience fear and I will face uncertainty. I will have OS!M after OS!M. That's the nature of leadership in the extreme: the dynamic interplay of love and fear. Acting out of love creates fear, and love gives me the courage to work through that fear."

"Love is the first part of Edg's leadership framework, too," I said, sounding like quite the organizational development weenie.

"Yeah. Edg's framework." Pops shot a smile at Edg. "You are one brilliant young man!"

I enjoyed the dynamics between the two of them, and I could feel that there was a rich history there. "I get the feeling that you've heard the LEAP thing somewhere before," I said.

"You could say that, yes. But love is not the first part of the framework; it's expressed *through* the framework. Here's the way I'd put it: *Love* generates *energy*, inspires *audacity*, and requires *proof*. LEAP, you see, is simply the Extreme Leader's active, dynamic expression of love."

"So it's *love* before you leap," I said. I received an enthusiastic cheer from my new friends.

"That's very good!" exclaimed the famous Mr. Maritime. "The Extreme Leader consciously and intentionally cultivates love in order to generate boundless energy and inspire courageous audacity. And he or she must provide the proof that it's all been worthwhile. Proof through the alignment between word and action, proof through the standing up for what's right, proof through measurable, tangible signs of progress, and proof through the experience of phenomenal success as well as glorious failure. That's the LEAP. And, if I can add to that, it's the LEAP that creates the OS!M. The OS!M is fear in the pursuit of creating something greater than the current reality. And the desire to create something greater is a bold expression of love. Simple as that."

Yeah. Simple as that.

■ ELEVEN

I had to admit that this love thing made a lot of sense to me. But, I also had to admit that the ghosts of a thousand executives seemed to be whispering, "Touchy-feeeeeely... touchy-feeeeeely," in my ear. I guess the haunting doubt showed on my face.

Edg jumped into the conversation, double-teaming me with his friend, Pops. "This goes directly to the bottom line. Love is just good business, dude. You know it from your own oh, let's call 'em *romantic adventures*."

"Come again," I said.

"Think back to your first date or two with that person you were really crazy about."

"You want me to think about a date?"

"Yeah. Stay with me for a minute. First of all, you really paid attention, didn't you? You listened intently to her every word, you noticed every detail: what she was wearing, what she ordered for dinner, and what songs she said she liked. And you took volumes of mental notes. You gathered data. And what did you do with that data?"

"I stalked her?"

"You responded; you acted. You delivered on her expressed desires and guessed at her unarticulated needs and responded to those, too."

"Were you there?"

"Not on your date, no. But I've been there myself. And so has anybody who has ever fallen in love."

I was beginning to think that maybe I wasn't so unique after all. What he said next confirmed it.

"So on the next date, you picked her up in that snappy Mustang of yours, but you left the top up because, even though you loved the feel of the wind whipping through the car, you remembered she told you how long it took her to get her hair just the way she liked it.

"At her door, you handed her one red rose, her favorite flower." He plucked one off a nearby bush for dramatic effect. "And, you escorted her on your arm to your waiting chariot."

"Am I that predictable?"

He smirked.

"So, what happened next, smart guy?"

"Then you headed for the opera house, because you knew she loved *La Traviata* and it happened to be in town, even though last week you thought *La Traviata* was an Italian restaurant and, frankly, still wished it were. Even though you'd rather see the Rolling Stones for the twentieth time, or get your teeth drilled by a very nervous dental student.

"But you also knew that your joy would come vicariously through hers. And your joy did indeed come when you saw those tenor-induced tears roll operatically down your sweetheart's cheek. Your joy came from the knowledge that you had done a very good thing and from the realization that you had won her heart."

Okay. So I had been to an opera or two over the years, and not because I'm a devotee of the genre. In fact, I don't think I'd ever chosen to go to anything where people said things like, "I'm a devotee of the genre," unless it was to please a loved one or impress an intended.

"Okay. You got me pegged, Edg. Guilty as charged. I'm a shameless, manipulative, conniving..."

"Hold on, Steve," Pops chimed in. "You're taking this the wrong way. This isn't about your dating rituals, this is about business."

"I'm not sure I'm tracking here," I said, feeling relieved that my love life had only been used metaphorically.

"Relationships in the world of business are won in analogous ways," Pops continued, "by paying nearly obsessive attention to the needs, desires, hopes, and aspirations of everyone who touches your business. By knowing not only when to stand firm on principle, there is such a thing as tough love, but also when to sacrifice some of your own short-term needs in order for us all to be successful in the long run. And by proving through your own actions that you really love your business, your customers, your colleagues, and your employees."

"You have to *prove* that you love the people at work?" My tone, I suspected, sounded a little more challenging than I had intended.

"This isn't some California, nutty granola, hoo-ha garbage," said Edg. "Saying that love has no appropriate place at work is like saying human beings have no appropriate place at work. It's nuts."

"I can feel the collective squirming of the entire human resources population," I said, hoping it would lighten things up. It didn't.

"Look," Edg continued, unabated, "you already bring your heart to work, and so does everybody else, right? It's not like you arrive at your office, pluck it out of your chest, and leave it throbbing on the sidewalk awaiting your return. So use it. If your heart is only performing an anatomical function, you are wasting one mighty fine organ."

"If you're not careful, you're going to miss the chance to let people know how much you care for them," said Pops. "The irony is that we often take for granted the very people that mean the most to us.

"It's like the story of the couple that had been married for 30 years. They're sitting around the breakfast table yet another morning, she with her coffee and he hidden behind his newspaper. She says to him, 'Honey, how come you never tell me that you love me anymore?' And he, from behind his newspaper, says, 'What do you mean? I told you I loved you when we got married. If anything changes, I'll let you know.' "

I chuckled, not only at the story but also at Pops's ability to tell it. He had great delivery.

"That's the way it is at work, too," Pops continued. "When someone does great work, you may give a pat on the back and say, 'Nice job.' But, if you don't take the time to stop, focus, and say how much you appreciate them, you end up wondering why they leave or run out of steam. So tell them now, right now, and don't wait another minute, because you never know when that next minute will be your last."

"So make sure to give timely recognition to the people you work with," I said. "With all due respect, Pops"—I was still having trouble calling him that—"that's the oldest management technique in the book."

He gave me a look that just about blew out the back of my head, and I got an immediate hit of the man's power. I suddenly realized, as if waking up from a daydream, that I had been lulled into thinking of this man as just a garden-loving, water-sipping, trailer-living, mellow and retiring Pops. But he wasn't. He was an empire builder. And, empires weren't built on a bunch of namby-pamby techniques.

He pushed his chair back and stood over me, never taking his eyes off mine.

"Once again, Mr. Farber," said W. G. Maritime, empire builder, "you have missed the point."

He turned away and disappeared into the trailer.

"What just happened there?" I asked Edg.

"He'll be back."

"Did I piss him off?"

"Just pushed a proverbial button, I think." He smiled and I felt better, though not much.

We sat and sipped our water in silence and, a few minutes later, Pops stepped out into the garden carrying a pad of paper and a book whose title I couldn't quite make out.

"*Band of Brothers*," said Pops as he settled back into his chair. "I want to read you something." He put the pad on the table and then leafed through the book.

"This is a letter written by Sergeant Floyd Talbert to his boss, Major Dick Winters, in 1945. Talbert had been wounded on the front lines of the war with Germany and was confined to his hospital bed when he wrote, 'Dick, you are loved and will never be forgotten by any soldier that ever served under you or I should say with you because that is the way you led—I would follow you into hell.'

"Now, I want you to tell me, Steve," he locked his eyes on mine again, "does that sound like a *management technique*?"

"Well, no. But..."

"Let's be clear about this. When Talbert said, 'I would follow you into hell,' he was not speaking metaphorically. He had already followed Winters into hell. Literally. And he would do it again. And for only one reason: love. Love of his country, love of his brothers, and love of his major."

He stopped, and the silence rushed in around us.

"Now, are you going to tell me that he was practicing a technique to get in good with his boss? That he was trying to kiss up, to manipulate the situation for his own future benefit? Is that what he was doing with this letter, Steve?"

"No."

"I have something for you," said Pops as he tore the top sheet from the notepad on the table.

It was a note to me from William Maritime written in a pointed, flowing script. Apparently, it's what he'd been doing when he went inside a little while ago. It said,

Dear Steve,

You and I have only just met, and I can already tell what an extraordinary person you are. Before you deny it, let me assure you that I am known throughout the world as an astute judge of character. Here's what I know about you, Steve: If you will allow yourself to remember why you became a leadership consultant, if you will let your heart recall the ideals that it once held as inviolable truth, if you will strive to express them in your own unique Farber voice, and if you will permit yourself the glorious experience of helping others in their journeys, you will touch the world in ways that will surpass your wildest imagination.

I, for one, would love to see it.

Love,

Pops

What happened next was a total and unexpected shock: my eyes welled up and a single, perfect, crystalline tear rolled off my face and splashed onto the paper.

"Thank you," I said.

It was all I could get out.

GET MY REWARD

2

■ TWELVE

We were saying our farewells out on the curb next to my Mustang. Pops had walked us out, and he was now warmly grasping my hand and giving me one last little gem of wisdom. And dropping one last bombshell.

"Well met, my friend," he said. "I won't forget this afternoon, and I hope you won't either."

"Not likely," I said. The note was folded neatly and tucked into the back pocket of my jeans, where it would stay until I changed pants. And then it would move right along with me, I already knew, to the next pair. I would carry that note as long as the paper held out. I was already having thoughts of lamination.

"I suspect that we won't be seeing each other again, Mr. Farber." He saw the disappointment on my face, I'm sure. I'd been secretly hoping that I'd just earned a new mentor, and secretly doubting that I deserved it.

"This little trailer is just a way station, of sorts. It's been a nice place to lay low and collect myself before moving on."

"Moving on to where?" I asked, suspecting that I wouldn't get an answer.

"Remember, Steve," he said, proving me right, "the Extreme Leader cultivates love, generates energy, inspires audacity, and provides proof. You have to fall in love with your life's work again, my friend, or your energy will wane, your voice will falter, and there will be nothing to prove but the fact that you're taking up valuable space. And, you won't be helping to develop and perpetuate the Extreme

Leadership that our fragile world so desperately needs right now.

"I challenge you to live up to this ideal:

Do what you love in the service of people who love what you do."

"I like the sound of that," I said.

"There are three parts: *Do what you love.* Make sure that your heart's in your work, and that you're bringing yourself fully and gratefully into everything you do. If you're not connected to your own work, you can't expect to inspire others in theirs. *In the service of people* will keep you true, honest, and ethical, at the very least. If you're doing what you love, you'll make yourself happy. But Extreme Leadership is not only about you; it's about your impact on others. *Who love what you do* doesn't mean that you just find the people who love you and then serve them; it means it's your responsibility to give everyone you serve something to love about you and what you're doing. See the difference, Steve?"

"Yes," I said. "I do."

"And you, my son," he turned to an uncharacteristically quiet Edg, "I will see later, right?"

"Oh, yeah, Pops. I'm on you like white on rice, like spots on dice."

"Like cold on ice, but twice the price," chimed Pops.

These guys had quite an act. I felt jealous, although I didn't need to.

"I love you, Pops," said Edg, and he gave him a hug and a tender kiss on the cheek.

Sensing my awkwardness at their unabashed display of affection, Pops turned to me.

"Okay. Hugs and kisses at work aren't always appropriate, I'll grant you that, but a son is allowed to kiss his father, isn't he?"

And then I got it: I had not only spent the afternoon with Pops and Edg, I'd spent it with W. G. Maritime and Son.

■ THIRTEEN

When one returns from a parallel universe, he or she often discovers that time stood still back in the real world. Apparently, judging by the blinking light on my telephone, I hadn't been in another, timeless dimension at all. The world had just kept chugging along.

I ignored the message light, stepped through the sliding glass doors of my apartment, and drank in the view from my porch. The darkening water of Mission Bay was starting to dance in the oncoming twilight as a light breeze stirred the palms.

I had a unique relationship with that palm tree at the end of the walkway. It was a sentry, watching out for me from its vantage point 80 feet up in the sky.

One morning, about a year earlier, I had woken up in a blue funk. I was impatient with myself and with my career, and I was more than a little bit lonely. Recently divorced and relocated to San Diego, I was trying to find my new identity as a 40-something single guy coming to terms with the apparent unreliability of matters of the heart. I was weathering a difficult time in my life, and this San Diego morning, sunny and breezy to the rest of the world, was bleak and stormy on this side of my eyeballs. So, I set out on what I hoped would be a therapeutic stroll in the reliably salty sea air.

I headed down the path and turned the corner onto the walkway alongside the bay, passing directly through the shadow of my towering palm. I had heard a loud clattering and, a split second later, felt a sudden and forceful thwack on the top of my head. A young couple sitting near the water jumped up and looked over at me in surprise.

I had almost lost my footing but managed to stay upright, even though I was a bit dizzy and disoriented. I looked down, and there by my feet on the sidewalk was a gigantic palm frond, its long, spindly fingers waving in the breeze in a mischievous gesture of greeting.

That son-of-a-bitch palm tree had staked me out. It had known my routine, waited for me to pass unwittingly into its target zone, and then with perfect marksman timing, from 80 feet up, it had let go one of its hands and smashed me on the head.

I had given a tentative wave to the couple to let them know that I was all right and offered an embarrassed laugh to acknowledge the absurdity of the scene that they had just witnessed.

Then I had looked up at the tree's remaining fronds, but they hadn't looked back and seemed, in fact, to look away suddenly so as not to be caught in the prank. "What? Is there a problem? I didn't do anything," is what I would have said had the roles been reversed.

Then I had noticed something truly odd. The day seemed brighter, and the breeze was invigorating; I felt good.

Sometimes it takes a smack from an old friend to snap you out of a deep funk. There was no law that said a new friend couldn't do that, too.

I was feeling like that again, standing there on my porch after spending several nearly surreal hours with Pops Maritime and Edg. Random meetings. Happenstance conversations. They all added up to one big, unexpected, exhilarating whack on the head.

The phone light was still blinking, and I paused for a moment to admire its persistence. It was time to renew my interest in the real world. The real world, however, didn't seem to be all that interested in me. One message.

It was Janice. "The 51% Guy has outdone himself. I'm *two seconds* away from walking out of this place. I made you a promise, though, and if you want to see me remain a woman of integrity, you'll get your butt to my office first thing in the morning." There was a slight pause. "Please?" her voice softened. She clicked off.

I felt an odd combination of flattery and annoyance as I listened to Janice's distress call. Flattered because she valued me enough to call me for help; annoyed because, frankly, I didn't feel like dealing with it right then. I was still trying to process all I had heard from my two new friends, and Janice's troubles were impinging on my reflective state of mind.

And then I noticed that I'd been unconsciously fingering a piece of paper in my back pocket. I pulled it out and read, "...*You will touch the world in ways that will surpass your wildest imagination.*"

"Yeah, I'll be there." I said to the machine. "Wouldn't have it any other way."

Friday

■ FOURTEEN

XinoniX headquarters were lodged in a growing cluster of biotech, Internet, and software companies in the Sorrento Valley area of San Diego. Many had hoped that this industrial neighborhood would turn out to be the epicenter of the coming biotech revolution. The recession had slowed things down a bit, but a lot of people remained hopeful. I was one of them, even though I had to admit that, as one who had struggled through physics and biology classes in school, the business of science was mystifying to me. But I didn't believe I had to understand something in order to be optimistic about its future. Sometimes intuition was enough.

I parked my valiant steed and walked through the automatic doors into the company's lobby. It's a tradition with this kind of company that no one shall pass the three-headed receptionist's guard station without an officially blessed and sanctioned security pass. Most of the passes say *escort required,* but they never live up to the promise in a way that would make it really interesting.

I signed the guest register and told the receptionist about my appointment with Janice. As I settled into the couch to await my liberation from corporate purgatory, I studied the XinoniX logo mounted prominently on the wall. The capital X on each end of the name was, I guessed, supposed to represent chromosomes. It made me think of Mexican beer.

XinoniX was also a palindrome—the same backwards as forwards. *Clever*, I was thinking, as Janice came through the security door. She was wearing designer jeans and a wool blazer over a simple off-white T-shirt. Casual, but confident: classic Janice. We gave each other a casual but confident hug and exchanged small talk as we walked down the hall past numerous pairs of curious eyes and ears.

We stepped into her office, and her demeanor shifted as she closed the door behind us. Something was off. She was crying.

She pulled herself together quickly, dabbing her eyes with a tissue that she plucked from a half-empty box on her desk. I kept quiet, not really out of respect, but because I had no idea what to say. Although Janice was a passionate and emotional person, teary displays were entirely out of character for her.

"Sorry," she said with resolve. "Have a seat, Steve."

"No need to apologize, Janice." I said as I lowered myself into an overstuffed chair. "Just tell me what's going on, and let's see if there's some way I can help."

"Okay, Doctor," she said wryly, her humor shooting through the gloom. She started pacing up and down in front of her desk as she caught me up on her latest encounter with Jeffers. She included every detail as though she'd rented the video and watched it several times. She wound up her account with a weary, "I've *had* it," and perched on the edge of her desk.

"Now what?" I asked. I get paid to ask the insightful questions.

"Now you help me figure out why I ought to stay."

I had no idea I was going to say it. It was as though a seed had been planted in my brain, and I didn't notice it until it launched this sprout from my mouth: "Why do you love this place, Janice?" I asked.

"Maybe you didn't hear what I just said. I don't love this place."

"Anymore."

"Right. Anymore."

"Then, why *did* you love this place?"

"The work we do is important."

"You're speaking in the present tense."

She stopped and considered the implication. "Yeah, it's still important."

"Why?"

"Because there's a great bunch of people here who have put in a lot of hours to make our products fly. They and their families have a lot at stake."

"That's true just about anywhere, isn't it?"

"Not like it is here. We develop software that scientists use to create new medicines."

"So?"

"What do you mean, *so?*"

"I mean there are a bunch of things a person of your talent can do. For someone of your caliber, a marketing plan's a marketing plan, once you learn the specifics of the business."

"This isn't just about marketing."

"No? What's it about, then?"

"It's about saving the world," she said without a hint of embarrassment.

I thought of my first conversation with Edg when he'd quoted Carly Fiorina: "A leader's greatest obligation is to make possible an environment where people can aspire to change the world." I assumed that Fiorina meant changing it for the better. Janice's agenda would qualify for that.

"So, you and your team are going to save the world. A bit lofty, isn't it?"

"Look," she said, pushing off from her desk, "500 years from now, the time we're living in is going to be remembered for two things." Her face flushed as the volume in her voice went up a notch. "Number one, we developed the technology to destroy the human race. And number two, we developed the technology to save the human race." She was almost shouting now.

"And I want *us* to be remembered for the technology that saved the human race. *That's* why this work is important."

"Well, there you go," I said. "Want me to help you draft a resignation letter?"

"Very funny," said Janice.

■ FIFTEEN

Love generates energy, but a few tacos also will do nicely in a pinch, I was thinking as I left the Jack in the Box and crossed Mission Boulevard.

I thought about my brief but powerful encounter with Janice earlier that day. She had forgotten why she loved her work and had just run out of steam. Once she remembered, her energy had come roaring back. It was an awesome thing to behold; right before my eyes she had summoned the juice to be an Extreme Leader at XinoniX, with or without the help of the 51% Guy.

After she threw the switch, so to speak, Janice had all but shoved me out of her office with an admonishment to "go find Teddy, like you promised." But not before she whispered "Thank you" with such gratefulness that I had felt wholly unworthy. I hadn't really done anything other than ask the right question at the right moment. And I hadn't even consciously known I was going to ask it.

Now, with my bag of tacos in hand, I was sauntering past the Mission Beach roller coaster and up to the boardwalk. The tourists and weekend beach bunnies had begun their migration, so the flow of pedestrian traffic was thick on this Friday afternoon.

I waited for an opening to traverse the busy walkway and finally found my opportunity in the short gap between a golden retriever pulling a skateboarder and a pack of three young ladies on Rollerblades. I dashed across the pavement, perched myself on the seawall, assumed the spectator position, and waited for Edg.

This was day two of my four-day commitment to him, and after yesterday's field trip to Pops's trailer, I was filled with anticipation. But I still had room for tacos.

As I munched taco number one, I thought about the mysterious Mr. Garrison. I hadn't yet done anything to try to locate the man, and I knew that Janice was hopeful that I'd be able to. While she and I were kindred spirits as far as hopefulness went, I didn't share her optimism in this instance.

After all, my sleuthing technique was severely limited. I had no clue how to proceed. I made a mental note to put in some kind of search time later that evening, which was my way of choosing to forget about it for the time being.

As I began to devour taco number two, I looked up the walkway and noticed that the board-pulling golden retriever was headed back in my direction. People were jumping out of the way to let the dog bound through, laughing as she passed. With tongue flapping and ears whipping in the wind, the skater pooch was the belle of the boardwalk, but her passenger was also having a grand time, grinning broadly, waving to the crowd, and hamming it up as he zipped on by. No surprise there, it was Edg.

"Hey!" he said when he saw me saluting. "Hop on!"

I wedged the taco in my mouth, clutched the bag in one hand, and jumped down off the seawall. I jogged alongside for a moment, put my free hand on Edg's shoulder and hopped onto the board, expecting to be whisked away at blazing speed.

The dog was healthy, no doubt, but she wasn't Superdog. The sudden addition of 200 pounds—all solid muscle, of course—to her load obviously exceeded her labor contract, and she went on strike. Immediately.

The dog slammed on her brakes, the board slammed into the dog, and Edg and I did an impromptu jazz dance over the dog and onto the pavement.

"You okay?" asked Edg.

"Mmmfifff," I said, as miraculously the taco was still lodged in my yap.

"Little OS!M there, dude?"

"More like an OF!M," I said as the dog tried to lick taco remnants from my face.

"The two of us were too much for Sadie, I guess," chuckled Edg as he pulled the retriever off of me.

Judging from her enthusiastic tongue wagging, Sadie, had she been a human, would have been chuckling, too. The saying, *happy as a clam*, applies to the entire golden retriever breed. It should be *happy as a pooch*, if you ask me.

I suggested that we take that happy pooch for a walk along the beach.

Edg handed his skateboard to an old guy with impressive dreadlocks who was sitting on the curb next to the lifeguard station. He said, "Thanks, Smitty," and motioned for me to follow him and Sadie down toward the water. Technically, this wasn't a dog beach, but no one, including the occasional member of the beach patrol, seemed to mind. Sadie, it appeared, had special privileges.

She pranced alongside of us and darted in and out of the surf, blissfully unaware that she was breaking the law.

We walked along in silence as I tried to sort out the questions about Edg that had been collecting in my head like so many bricks. They weren't stacking neatly. I was just about to launch into my interrogation when Edg motioned for me to keep quiet. He gestured toward Sadie.

"Watch her," he said.

As though on cue, the overgrown golden retriever took off up the beach kicking up little puffs of sand as she ran. She swung a wide arc to the left and headed straight into the ocean at full speed. She bounded over the first couple of small waves, and as the water deepened, she paddled furiously until a formidable mother of a wave crashed down over her body.

I gasped reflexively as Edg laughed. Sadie's head popped up out of the surf, and she propelled herself back toward the shore with professional ease. It was as close to body surfing as a dog could come, I figured. She sprinted out of the water and shook herself vigorously, sending a spray of fine mist in every direction.

Don't let anyone tell you that dogs don't smile. She was grinning like a child, no doubt about it, as she trotted back to us.

"Does she ever stop?" I asked.

"Not out here she doesn't. She loves the beach. And when Sadie's in love, Sadie's unstoppable."

"Wait, don't tell me," I said.

Edg's right eyebrow arched slightly as he looked at me. "Don't tell you what?"

"Love generates energy, right?"

"Guess I didn't have to tell you. To put it simply, the more love you have, the more energetic you are," Edg said, his words punctuated by Sadie's enthusiastic and expectant panting. "Without it, you're a drone."

He threw a stick of driftwood into the ocean, and Sadie took off after it like a shot. A few minutes later she was back, dripping with seawater. She dropped the stick at Edg's feet and looked up into his eyes.

"What do you think will happen if I throw the stick again?"

Sadie wiggled and danced around us, answering the question in doggie body language.

"I'll go out on a limb and guess that she'll fetch it."

He threw. She fetched. And here she was again, a big, wet, furry déjà vu.

"How long do you think she'll keep doing it?" he asked as he let the stick fly. "Forever," he said, answering his own question. He was looking out over the ocean as he tossed and talked. He stopped suddenly and turned to look at me.

"You know why she'll keep coming back?" he asked.

"Why?"

"Because she's a dog."

He paused to let the profundity sink in. It didn't.

"And?" I asked.

"Kinky Friedman said, 'Money can buy the dog, but only love can make it wag its tail.' A stick is motivation enough for Sadie because, to her, there are few activities she loves more than the fetch game."

"And?" I repeated.

"Look," he said, "I know it's simplistic, but the point is people are not dogs; we're not content to spend our lives chasing sticks. We're far more complex than that, yet so many businesspeople throw sticks and expect others to fetch and come back again and again like good little doggies."

"I think it's safe to say that you've completely lost me."

"At work, if you want talented people to keep coming back, what do you do? Besides pay them, of course."

"You mean how do you energize and inspire the masses?" He nodded, so I answered my own question. "Most people will give a series of fist-pumping speeches, write rousing memos, print T-shirts, that kind of stuff."

"Right," said Edg. "But you're still missing the biggie."

"You mean the vision thing?"

"Bingo!" He chucked the stick, and Sadie bolted there and back again. "It's become conventional wisdom that in order to get people excited about the present, you talk about the future. You have a vision statement. Problem is, most vision statements are way too incomplete at best, and cynicism-inducing claptrap at worst."

"Agreed," I agreed.

He chucked the stick again. "It's easy to pump people up, but it's usually a temporary phenomenon. Michael Cunningham, the novelist, said, 'If you shout loud enough for long enough, a crowd will gather to see what all the noise is about. It's the nature of crowds. They don't stay long, unless you give them reason.'"

"Well said," I said.

"Leaders ostensibly use vision statements to give people reason, right?" Once more, he chucked the stick.

"And you're saying they don't?" I asked, feigning shock.

"Not hardly." He waited for Sadie to return, and when she did he told her to sit and then scratched her aggressively behind the ears.

"First of all, every business book you pick up will tell you that you need to have a vision statement, so any company that's done its required reading will have one. It develops like this: A group of senior executives, now known as the executive team, goes away on an off-site, sits down together and has a poetry contest. They try to hammer out just the right words and phrases, and they argue for hours—days, sometimes—over the choice of words. 'Should we call them *customers* or *clients*, are they *shareholders* or *stakeholders*, do we have *employees* or are they *associates*?' They tear their hair out, and they threaten, and they fight, and ultimately, at the end of the day, they have created a magnificent document, and they're so, so proud. So what do they do?"

"Get drunk?"

"They laminate it. Laminate it on little wallet-sized cards and hand out a copy to everybody in the organization. Then they hang a full-color calligraphy version in the reception area and wait for something to happen. After a time, they look around the company and are absolutely incredulous that nothing has changed. 'What the hell is wrong with these people?' they exclaim. 'Can't they read?'

"It's as if they expect the laminated card to work like a nicotine patch. Carry it close to your skin and the energy will somehow get into your bloodstream. It doesn't happen that way. Most corporate vision statements are generic and meaningless to the very people they are supposed to inspire. And they don't, to say the least, generate energy of any kind.

"They may as well say, 'Blah, blah, blah, blah, *company*. Blah, blah, blah, blah, *customers*. Blah, blah, blah, blah, *shareholders*. Blah, blah, blah, blah, *employees*.' " He threw the stick, and there went Sadie.

"It's simply a case of mistaken cause and effect," Edg continued. "A vision statement doesn't generate energy, love does, great ideas do, principles and values do. A vision statement that comes from a workshop exercise is usually about as energizing and memorable as a saltine cracker."

I'd witnessed that scenario over and over. One senior team of executives at a bank I had worked with did *The Vision Off-site* and came away with their very own snappy acronym: STAR. I can't remember what it stood for; I think it was service, teamwork, accountability, and respect. Or maybe it was synergy, tenacity, ability, and returns. What I do remember is that their frontline folks kept telling me they were confused about the organization's vision.

So, I went back to the executive team and I said, "Listen, I've got some feedback for you. Your employees are telling me they don't understand the vision of the company." That infuriated one of the senior executives, whose face turned so red that I thought his head was going to pop right off.

"What do you mean they don't understand the vision?" he had howled. "We did that! It's STAR!"

"Well," I had said gently, "the very fact that you are saying we did that means that you are *not doing* that. Maybe your folks need a little more than an acronym."

"Like what?" he had demanded.

"How about an anagram?" I had suggested. He hadn't appreciated my wry humor as much as I had, even though RATS was, I had pointed out, a great anagram for STAR.

"But vision from the heart is, by definition, an expression of love," Edg was saying. "And not only is that more energizing, it *is* energy. It's juice, man." He looked out over the ocean as Sadie bolted, once again, into the surf.

"Martin Luther King's 'I Have a Dream' speech was juice for a generation. He didn't have to hand out 250,000 laminated cards at the Lincoln Memorial on that hot August day in 1963. Watch the tape, it was pure energy. Juice. Life itself." He called to Sadie, and we turned around and headed back toward the lifeguard station.

He looked down at the sand as we walked. "Think about your clients, Steve. I'll bet the vast majority of them grossly underestimate the power of their own hearts. They have no freakin' idea how much energy they can unleash in themselves and those around them if they just put down that bureaucratic, banal, generic crapola and tell people why they love their businesses, and communicate their authentic hopes and aspirations for the future of their companies. Am I right?"

I flashed back to the scene in Janice's office. "I suspect so," I said. "So what's the remedy for the 'blah, blah, blah' corporate vision statements?"

"Burn the damned things," said Edg.

"Isn't that a bit harsh?" I asked. "What's next? Flags and bras?"

He let out a deep breath. "*Love generates energy* is our premise, right?" He drew a heart in the sand with the toe of his sandal. I remembered when my daughter was six, and we were visiting San Diego from our home in the landlocked Iowa countryside. On the beach one day, she'd surrounded herself with hearts that she'd traced in the wet sand. I still had a picture of it nearly 20 years later. She had been sitting, I realized with a sudden electric jolt, on the very same beach where Edg and I now stood. I shook myself and tried to concentrate on the present. Edg drew a second heart, then a third and a fourth, and he kept going until we were standing in the middle of a circle of hearts.

"The Extreme Leader's job," said Edg, "is to connect all those hearts, true?"

"Ideally," I said.

"No. Not ideally. Absolutely. Without that heart connection, you may have an employer/employee thing going on or a bureaucratic boss/subordinate relationship. People who don't have that heart connection won't try to change the world together. And if you're not trying to change the world, you haven't entered the realm of the Extreme Leader.

"And that, then, begs the question of how to establish the connection."

"So how do you establish the connection?" I asked, since he'd begged.

"By revealing yourself as a human being to those you hope to lead. So instead of reciting a vision statement, feel the intent of that statement, reflect on the ideals that it represents and take it all into your own heart. Then at every opportunity, whether you're talking one-on-one or standing in front of a crowd, you say, in essence, 'This is who I am, this is what I believe, this is what I think we can do together if we put our hearts into it. Look at how magnificent our future can be. Please join me and let's help each other make this happen.' Then you can burn the document because, in effect, you've *become* the vision."

"That's rare," I said. "I'm not really sure I've seen anyone do that in business."

"I've seen it," said Edg. "And the connection is electric."

"Energy," I said.

"Generated straight from the heart."

■ SIXTEEN

Smitty was still on his perch watching the boardwalk traffic from behind his large, yellow-tinted glasses. Sadie ran up to him and pushed her snout under his hand.

"Sadie, Sadie, beautiful lady! How's my girl?" said Smitty, as he lowered his head and turned it to give the dog access to his ear, which she licked enthusiastically. "Did you enjoy your jaunt with Uncle Edg?" Sadie said, *Oh, yes, I sure did*, but not in those words.

"Steve, Smitty. Smitty, Steve," said Edg as he took back his skateboard from his dreadlocked pal. "Why don't you guys get acquainted? I'll be back in a flash."

Before I could protest, Edg was pushing away on his board.

"Have a seat, man." Smitty patted the curb. His dreadlocks fell around a face that sprouted the most impressive beard I'd ever seen up close. It was a ZZ Top sort of thing, but red and not as tame. His hair was so outrageous, in fact, that I found myself wondering if it was real. Smitty's head was a hirsute funhouse.

"He may be a while or he may not be back at all. One can never tell with Mr. E." His voice was raspy, and he spoke with a watered-down Texas drawl, evidence that he had once had an accent as thick as barbecue sauce.

"Sadie's your dog?" I asked, as I lowered myself to the curb.

"Not really sure who belongs to who," said Smitty.

"She's a beauty."

"She knows it; that's for damn sure. She gets a lot of attention on account of it, too." Sadie wagged her body. "But she's happy to share some of that with me. Ain't ya, pooch?"

Almost on cue, a flock of young ladies stopped on the boardwalk in front of us to fawn and coo over the dog.

Smitty offered a couple of hi theres and howdys, and the girls were polite enough to vaguely acknowledge his existence. He sat grinning through his beard like the sun shining through a hedge.

"Ah, yes," he sighed as he watched the flock flutter away. "Life is full of wonderful little exclamation points, ain't it?"

I assumed that the question was rhetorical.

"Ain't it?" he repeated, annihilating my rhetorical question theory.

"Yeah. Okay, I never quite thought of it that way, I guess."

"Yep. It's true. Exclamation points, question marks, asterisks... everywhere you look." He scanned the boardwalk through his yellow lenses.

Curiouser and curiouser, I thought, ignoring Smitty's blabbering. There was no sign of Edg; he had all but dumped me and taken off with no explanation, request, or instruction.

"So... Smitty," I said. "How do you know Edg?"

"Edg, Edg, Edg, how do I know Edg?" He grinned. "Well, I used to work with him, that's how."

My heart jumped a bit. I was about to hear an actual detail, a bona fide fact about Edg's past. "Doing what?" I asked, probably sounding too eager.

"Oh... this and that, I guess. When there was stuff that needed doing, I did it."

"Yeah, but what kind of stuff?" I was rapidly losing patience.

He paused for a split second. Then he said, "Oh, hell. It really don't matter. It was just a bunch of technical titty twistin', really. Point is, he made me a very rich man."

That was quite a punch line. I tried not to look surprised, which was about as easy as trying not to look like I obeyed the laws of gravity.

"And that is what allowed me to get started in my new line of work," Smitty continued, as though he'd said something as banal as "I scratch myself."

"Which is what?" I asked.

"I'm in the sign business." It sounded like, *sahn*.

"You make signs?" I asked.

"Nope."

"Then, what?"

"I read them."

"I'll show you what I mean," Smitty said, apparently in response to the way my face had scrunched up into one of his environmental question marks.

He got up and started walking with Sadie along the boardwalk toward the surf-and-skate shop on the corner across from Canes.

"Look there." He pointed, stretching out his tanned, sinewy arm.

The cement lamppost was plastered with papers and graffiti. A bold bumper sticker reading, *No Fear*, was posted just above a flyer for a speed metal band called *Satan's Bastard Goat Child*.

"Good words of encouragement on that sticker, don't ya think?" he said.

"Excellent," I acknowledged. "Especially if you're going to that concert."

"How about this?" He put his arm around another pole, which supported a sign that said *Unattended vehicles will be towed at the owner's expense*. "It's a fact of life just as sure as shit, right?"

"Meaning?" I asked.

"A lot of folks out there," he spread his arms to indicate the beach crowd, "are unattended vehicles. Four wheels, a chassis, and no driver. Nobody there to put the top up in a rainstorm. No sense, in other words, of *who* they are. Just tooling along and hoping someone will jump in and put 'em in gear before they get towed to the auto pound."

"That's a rather grim view of humanity," I said to Smitty the Sign Reader.

"Ah, c'mon. It's not grim or jolly. It's just the way it is, unattended vehicles will be towed. So... *attend*. That's just good advice, ain't it, Sadie?"

"Curb your dog," I said, quoting the famous sign.

"Now you're gettin' it! Great advice! It's all around us. We're surrounded by lessons; we just need to notice the signs and ask the right questions. Ask the right questions and you learn some pretty good stuff about what's goin' on around you. And when you realize that there's deep significance in seemingly insignificant things, the whole world pops to life, and everything becomes part of a 24/7/365 multidimensional, hyperaccelerated, interactive learning laboratory."

"Really." It sounded like a statement, but I meant it as a question. "What about that sign?"

"*No parking*," read Smitty. "That's pretty obvious, ain't it?"

"Or that T-shirt?"

"'*Skate or die*,'" He recited. "Just another version of *No parking*, don't ya think? Keep moving; don't stand still. Life is movement; stagnation is death. No parking, skate or die."

I felt a slight chill. "So you're saying that there are messages everywhere?" I asked.

"Not really. Truth be told, all the messages are in one place... right here." He tapped himself on the head. "It's all in the interpretation, right? To most people, *yield* is only a traffic sign, but to me, it's a lesson about going with the flow, get it? Same sign, different meaning. The sign's just a stimulant. The difference is what I see in the sign, how I read it. The difference is right here in my itty-bitty brain. The sign just gets me to payin' attention."

"So, read signs and interpret their meaning," I mused.

"Yep. Read the sign, ask yourself what the lesson is, and you'll get you some wisdom at every turn. Let me show you one of my all-time favorites." He said it like *fay-vo-rites*.

Sadie and I followed Smitty up the boardwalk. He moved with surprising speed, cutting back and forth through the crowd. I had to trot to keep up, but Sadie never broke a sweat. Dogs never do.

About a half-mile up the walk was a beachside strip mall with several shops, restaurants, a few offices, and a public restroom. I followed Smitty through a door that said *Men*, while Sadie, apparently a good sign reader herself, waited for us outside. Smitty opened a stall, and I headed for the other apparatus mounted on the wall.

"Wait," he said. "I want to show you something."

"Excuse me?"

"Nooo, no, no!" he laughed, picking up on my suspicious tone. "I want to show you the quintessential, classic management sign."

"In that stall?"

"In this and untold others."

I walked over slowly, pulling the sunglasses off my face so my eyes could adjust to the restroom's dim light. I poked my head inside the stall.

"There it is," said Smitty.

Expecting to see the graffiti equivalent to *mybosssucks.com*, I scanned the stall walls for anything of organizational significance. Other than a few phone numbers and testimonials to someone's ability to impart on me a good time, I saw nothing of note.

"You're looking in the wrong place—it's not graffiti," he said.

And then I saw it. And it wasn't the first time I'd seen it, either. It was just the first time I'd paid attention. Screwed to the wall over the toilet was a seat-cover dispenser with a notice that read:

Provided by the Management for Your Protection

"That, m'friend," Smitty said, "is the single most dangerous management myth of all time."

"Really," I said, once again making a question sound like a statement.

"Yup. First off, it's a lie: you will never, *never* see one of them ole management boys wrapped in a tool belt and screwing seat-cover dispensers into the stall wall. It's a facilities staffer that's covering your butt, not the management. In fact, the custodians of this building provide for the *management's* protection, not the other way around."

"So you're saying that it's not literally true."

"Yeah, sure, I'm sayin' that. But it's the attitude that really puts a barb in my bony backside."

"The sign has an attitude?"

"Yeah, man. It's arrogant. It's overinflated, self-indulgent, and pitifully self-important. Management, the benevolent protector. Management, the bestower of blessings. Management, the big mommy/daddy. What a load... pun intended.

"All you gotta do is read the business alphabet from Andersen to Xerox to see that it's a lie. In business, nobody provides for your protection. Except you."

"What do they call you, Smitty the Cynic?"

I followed him out of the stall, out of the men's room, and back out into the sunshine.

"I am not a cynic. Not by a Texas long shot. I'm just callin' it like I see it." He whistled for Sadie.

"You're saying it's not management's job to protect its employees. Your friend Edg, though, says that love is at the foundation of good business. So you guys disagree?"

"We're in picture-perfect agreement, as a matter a fact. There are different kinds of love, m'friend. A business should be socially responsible and ethically minded and all that good stuff. That's a kind of love, ain't it? And it should love its employees for devoting talent, time, and energy to the biz, and it should show it. But a business also has a responsibility to itself, it's gotta stay healthy. And sometimes that means makin' decisions and doin' things that'll piss some of its employees off. So don't it follow that all of us, as individuals, have to take responsibility for ourselves? We can't abdicate our personal responsibility to some supposed higher authority.

"Look around you, man. Forget the accounting scandals for a minute; do you see any *legitimate* companies that'll give you a job for life? Nope. Ever see anyone with piles of talent who lost a job? Yup. Happens every day, no matter what condition the economy's in. Sometimes love for the health of the company and love for individual employees smack right up against each other. Sometimes love hurts, and sometimes it's got nothing to do with personal love at all."

"Well, the world's changing, the market's changing, and some of those things are just unavoidable," I said. "They're beyond any one human's control."

"That's all I'm sayin', friend," agreed Smitty. "Nobody, not your friend, not your minister, not your rabbi, not your mullah, not your momma, and certainly not your management, is going to protect you from the big, wild world. And you know why?"

"I'm pretty sure."

"Because they can't. What they can do, what they should do, what they damn well better do, if they have an ounce of gray matter, is create an environment where people can thrive as adults and grow as leaders."

"Where people can aspire to change the world," I offered.

"Yessir! And, if and when you leave the company, you are more capable and experienced than the day you started. This ain't about protecting you from the world; it's about giving you the chance and means to change it.

"So, two things gotta happen, the way I see it. First, management has to stop pretending that they want to be your momma. They can start by taking down all them bathroom signs, and then we'd put up ones that say something like:

> These covers are provided to you by a member of the facilities crew who works all day in a thankless job. Management doesn't even know how these got here, but we're sure they'd approve, because we all sit here eventually. With these seat covers, you have an opportunity to protect yourself. We recommend that you take it. After all, it's your ass."

I stared at him. "What a great metaphor," I said.

"But that's only the first part," he continued, ignoring my compliment. "Yeah, management has to stop pretending to be the great protector, but the rest of us have to stop askin' and expectin' them to be. We gotta get over the whole idea of *them*, as a matter of fact. We need to hold ourselves accountable and stop looking to blame *them* when things go wrong."

I knew he was right, of course. In every seminar I had ever taught, in every company and at every level, the subject of *them* always emerged, but I asked for an example anyway.

"Example? Well, it's universal. Sure as the sun will rise in the east, folks will end up blaming their woes on *them*. Managers blame their woes on *them*, the employees, and employees gripe about *them*, the management. Presidents and CEOs whine about *them*, the board, or *them*, the analysts, and we all moan about *them*, the shareholders. The conversation goes round and round like a Ferris wheel, and pretty soon you're not sure who's talking about who.

"Look, man, say that you're the management."

"Okay," I complied.

"And say, for example, you've just distributed another employee opinion survey. You ask *them* for their candid views on the company, but 70% of *them* don't respond. So you complain about how unresponsive *they* are, and then you ignore the feedback of the other 30%. With me so far?"

"Seen it a thousand times," I said.

"*They*, consequently, start talking about *you* or *them* as you're known to *them*, and how *you*, or *they* as you are known to *them*, don't really care about what *we*, or *they*, as they're known to *you*, have to say about *them*, or *you* as you're known to yourself. Still with me?"

"Here comes lunch."

"And where does it all end up? What's the big conclusion? 'They will never change,' they say about them."

"The classic organizational stalemate," I said.

"And it's all an illusion."

"Meaning?"

"There ain't no *they*."

"There ain't?"

"Nope. There's just *us*," He whistled for Sadie again. "She headed home, I guess."

"Not counting on you to provide for her protection, I take it."

"Even the dog gets it," said Smitty.

It was late and I was hungry, and after he declined my invitation to a steak dinner, Smitty and I said our good-byes. He walked south toward the lifeguard station where we'd met, and I headed north and away from this very unusual character.

With a vague rumbling in my stomach and a wisp of a smile on my face, I walked up Mission Boulevard toward the restaurant. I had a lot to think about from my brief and bizarre conversation with Smitty: them versus us, protection versus self-reliance, blame versus accountability. At times, I admitted to myself, I did hope that someone would protect me. That someone would take a deep, personal interest in my well-being. That someone would lead me in my life. It just sounded so much easier than the alternative which, I realized, was being a leader myself.

I looked up and saw a sign posted outside a small retail shop.

No loitering, it read.

"Hmm," I mused. "Wonder what that means."

MY

GET

REWARD

3

■ SEVENTEEN

All signs pointed to the fact that I deserved a big steak. That's why I soon found myself sitting in a small booth at Saska's Steakhouse, a Mission Beach landmark since God created cows. I looked around the small, dark dining room as I chewed on a tender piece of something that had once chewed its cud. The Christmas lights, which are a year-round fixture at Saska's, sparkled from beam to beam. My gaze traced a pathway starting at a brass-framed mirror, moved down the glittered wall to an indiscernible velvet painting, jumped over a couple of booths, and landed, finally, on the small, flickering candle flame cupped in a red jar in the middle of my table. I suddenly remembered what I needed to do. As I borrowed the White Pages from the bartender, I explained that it was dinner reading.

The brilliant detectives always start with the obvious, which is exactly why I had overlooked it. Why not see whether the elusive Mr. Garrison was listed?

He was. Hidden cleverly in the G section.

I fired up my cell phone and dialed the number. The phone rang twice, and I hung up, realizing that I'd given no thought to what I'd say when he—or worse yet, his voice mail—answered. Better to think it through first.

I collected my thoughts into a relatively coherent form and dialed the number again. A woman's voice said: "You've reached the number of Teddy Garrison. You may think that this is an answering machine. It is not. This is a questioning machine. And there are two questions: Who are you? and What do you want? And lest you think those are trivial questions, consider that most people go through their entire lives without ever answering either one." Beeeep.

The recording threw me. I'd heard that message before from my friend, Terry Pearce, who'd written about it in his book, *Leading Out Loud*. Whether Garrison had also read Terry's book, or he'd come up with the same message on his own, it was still another odd and increasingly irritating coincidence. Either way, it made my synapses misfire, which, in turn, sent my words spluttering off into oblivion.

"Um. Ha-ha. That's really very clever," I stammered. "Who am I? Well, I'm Janice's friend. I'm... I'm more than that, certainly, but in this context that's the important thing."

Idiot, I said to myself.

"What do I want? For you to call me back. That's it, really. That's it for now, I mean. There's a lot more that I want out of *life*, if that's what you're asking, but for right now a quick conversation with you about Janice and her future at XinoniX would make my day. Not that my day is important to you, I understand."

Genius, I said to myself with withering, silent sarcasm.

I left my number and signed off.

"I hate voice mail," I said, unrecorded and to no one in particular.

As I left the restaurant, I pulled in a deep draught of the sea air. The Mission Beach area of San Diego is a thin peninsula of land, five or six blocks wide, between the Pacific Ocean and Mission Bay. While the ocean side with its boardwalk and crowds is crazy and chaotic, the bay side is quiet and serene, an ideal place to walk when in a quiet and reflective mood. That's exactly where I found myself, so I crossed Mission Boulevard, cut through the lobby of the Catamaran Hotel, walked out to Mission Bay, and headed south toward my apartment.

Dusk had settled in and sounds of distant laughter and music bounced at me from across the water to remind me that I was spending another Friday evening alone. I think it was Nelson Mandela who said, as he emerged, blinking, into the bright daylight of freedom after spending some ungodly amount of time in solitary confinement, "Loneliness sucks."

In the 45 minutes it took me to walk home, I managed to spiral myself into a deeply melancholy state of mind. Humming a mournful Hank Williams tune to myself, I unlocked the door and stepped inside. What moved? Was someone in here? "Wishful thinking," I half joked to myself.

Something brushed against my leg, and I jumped and shouted "HEY!" at a pitch much higher than, in retrospect, I care to admit. In moments like that, the imagination goes into hyperdrive and conjures up all kinds of horrible and grotesque possibilities. The reality, in this case, was just a little brown kitty cat rubbing up against my shin.

Apparently, it had come up the back steps, jumped over the railing, and ventured in through an open window. Now it was meowing at me, as though I owed it a plate of tuna for its remarkable efforts.

"Hey, little kitty," I managed to say in spite of the thunderous pounding in my chest, "you are in a no-animal zone. You trying to get me evicted?" I didn't expect it to answer, and fortunately, it didn't. But when it turned and headed back for the window, I noticed what appeared to be a folded piece of paper taped to its small, brown collar. Instinctively, I bent down for a closer look and there, much to my surprise, written in blue marker was my name. "Fan mail from some flounders?" I said in my best Bullwinkle voice, as I plucked the paper from around her neck.

Relieved of her duty, the little courier jumped up on the window ledge and bolted into the night.

"This is not normal," I muttered to myself as I unfolded the paper. "It's usually a cow that comes through my window to deliver mysterious notes. Or a yak." I sat down at the dining room table, laid the note down, and smoothed out the creases. Two pages.

"*Dear Steve,*" the note began in a flowing, pointy script. "*Please excuse the unorthodox delivery method, but I've never been a subscriber to convention. Earlier this evening you left a message for me; now I have one for you.*"

■ EIGHTEEN

This didn't add up. Forget the apparent fact that Garrison knew who I was, but how the hell did he know where I lived? And what about his seeming preternatural ability with animals, felines, anyway. Was he running some kind of mammalian messenger service?

I ran over to the window where the cat had just perched and peered down into the dark street. Empty. I had hoped, I guess, to see the dark and mysterious silhouette of Teddy Garrison lurking in the shadows of the alley. It wasn't going to be that easy.

I took a deep breath, a decent alternative to letting out an anxious wail, and went back to the table, sat, and read the note at least a dozen times:

"I know your concern for Janice is heartfelt. I know this because she has told me about you from time to time, and you've always sounded like a good coach and friend, and the two go hand in hand. So I hope you'll understand me when I say that I left XinoniX not for me, but for her.

"My mentor once said to me that you need to love the people or you'll lose the game. Love, contrary to the popular, romantic notion, is not all hearts and flowers. Love, oftentimes, looks, feels, and hurts like a son of a bitch. Especially in business.

"I don't only love Janice as she is today; I love what she's capable of becoming. Problem is, she'll never become it as long as I'm around for her to lean on. Janice is the future of the company; she just doesn't know it yet. And when I found myself in the position of having more confidence in Janice than she had in herself, I saw my resignation as my ultimate leadership opportunity.

"Mostly, leadership requires extreme personal engagement, but sometimes it demands an act of self-removal. This is one of those times. If that makes me look—for the time being, anyway—like a cowardly, selfish schmuck, then so be it.

"I know she thinks I've thrown her into the Jeffers den to be eaten alive. Bob has a reputation as a brutal autocrat, and he appears to be the antithesis of the very XinoniX culture that Janice worked so hard to help create. Appearances are misleading.

"Jeffers is a brilliant strategist and a superb executive. In other words, he not only plans well, but he also executes the plan, whatever it is, with precision, speed, and focus—all necessary and crucial qualities for the company's next phase. As a leader of people, though, he's awful. That's where Janice comes in.

"Janice and Jeffers are perfect for each other and the company. But this is more like an arranged marriage than love at first sight, and I'm the arranger. I would never be able to convince them of their value to each other; they'll have to discover that for themselves. I believe they will. Right now, Janice sees it as a war.

"But she doesn't need to conquer Bob, she needs to win him. Help her to see the difference, Steve, and you'll be doing her the favor of a lifetime.

"As for me, I hope I've left enough of myself in the company's DNA, as it were, so that it will continue to evolve in the way I hope and envision.

"As for Janice, this is her moment to shine as an Extreme Leader.

"As for Jeffers, this is his moment to learn from his weaknesses.

"And as for you, Mr. Farber, it's decision time. You need to choose. Are you going to play around or put your skin in the game? That sounds cryptic, I know. Just consider this to be another piece of your own leadership puzzle. You figure out where it fits."

It was signed, simply,

"*Teddy.*"

Saturday

■ NINETEEN

That night, I dreamed I was having espresso and maple scones with Teddy Garrison. He was sitting at such an angle that I couldn't clearly see his face, but his profile was familiar, as was the sound of his voice.

"How did you find me?" I was asking the side of his head.

"That's the wrong question," he mumbled through a mouthful of pastry, spraying a few crumbs for emphasis.

"What's the right question?" I asked.

"That is," said Ted the dream.

I awoke on Saturday morning to the sound of thunder. As it turned out, it wasn't thunder, exactly, but someone pounding on my door. I did my best to ignore the intruder, who was doing his best to make sure that he couldn't be ignored. I shook the cobwebs from my dream filled brain and fumbled for my jean shorts, which were positioned strategically in a pile on the floor next to my bed.

I stumbled through the apartment and past the table where the note still lay, rippling slightly in a breeze wafting in through the open window. As I yanked the door open, I expected to see Bruce, the landlord, who lived upstairs, or maybe a cat with a telegram. It was neither.

"Morning, Sunshine," said Edg.

"You're not a cat," I said.

"Nowadays we say dude," he said, without missing a beat.

"Don't take this the wrong way," I said. "But what the hell are you doing here?"

He held up a white bag in his left hand. "Sustenance," he said as he pushed past me. I followed him into my own apartment.

He put the bag on the table next to Garrison's note and started poking around the kitchen. "Where do you keep the morning elixir?"

I ground some mocha java beans, and Edg filled the coffeepot with purified water from the jug on the counter. The apartment filled with a beautiful, caffeinated aroma, and my head, finally, began to clear itself of the murky effects of dream, sleep, and rude awakening.

We sat facing each other across the table. "Here's the question of the day, Edg."

"Fire away."

"I've never told you where I live, so how did you find me?"

"Why is that the question of the day?"

"Long story. Answer, please."

He opened the little white bag and pulled out a chocolate croissant. "I'm going to let you in on a little secret." He tore the pastry into two and handed me the bigger piece. I took the offering and leaned forward in my chair.

He paused, as if contemplating whether or not to let me in on his special technique. "It's like this," he said, locking his eyes on mine. "*You're in the phone book, dude!*"

He let out a loud guffaw, obviously in response to the disappointed look on my face. The mystery had evaporated in a puff.

He opened the bag again and placed a fresh scone on the table. Given the dream I'd just had, this was a Rod Serling moment.

"That's not maple, is it?"

"Blueberry. Here, take half."

"No thanks. I'm not in a scone mood."

"C'mon, take it. I never scone alone."

I obliged.

A gust blew through the window, and Garrison's note fluttered off the table and landed near my feet. I picked it up, folded it, and slid it under my coffee cup. I was trying to be inconspicuous, but I let my gaze linger just a little too long.

"Writing love notes?" Edg grinned. "Or getting them?"

"Neither," I said curtly, hoping he'd drop the inquisition. I didn't want to explain this odd note and the odd circumstances around it. I couldn't. It made very little sense, at least in the normal, rational sort of way that things are supposed to. But then neither did Edg nor the circumstances around him, me, Pops, and, most recently, Smitty. So, *what the hell*, I figured.

I told Edg the whole story starting with Janice's phone call. I talked about my visit to her office, her challenge with

Jeffers, and her subsequent epiphany about the purpose of her work. I told how she'd asked me to find this Garrison guy, and how he'd found me instead. I told about the cat, the note—I waved the evidence in the air for emphasis—and even the dream. He stopped chewing and looked down at his half-eaten scone.

"Hmm," he offered. He tapped his fingers on the table. "Should we play 20 questions, or are you gonna let me read the note?"

I handed it to him, and he took his time soaking it in. He read it silently two or three times, stopped, gazed up at the ceiling, looked at me, and read it again.

"Well?" I prompted.

Edg folded the note, handed it back to me, and shoved the last piece of scone into his mouth. "Awesome," he said with a mouthful. "Let's go."

He jumped up and headed for the door.

I, of course, followed.

■ TWENTY

This field trip brought us into the Point Loma neighborhood of San Diego: old money residents, brick-and-mortar houses, and tree-lined streets. Following Edg's directions, I curbed the Mustang in front of an impressive Tudor-style home. Deep green vines of ivy formed an archway over its stained glass door.

"Guess where we are," said Edg.

"No clue."

"I'll give you one: 'Go to the source and ask the horse, he'll give you the answer that you endorse,'" he sang. "'That is, of course, unless the horse is the famous...'" He left the melody hanging and waited for me to finish it.

"Mister Ed?" I said. "Mister Ed the talking horse lives here?"

"Close. How about Mr. Ted?"

"Come again?"

"This, my good man," he said, slipping into a mock British accent, "is the illustrious domicile of one Theodore 'Teddy' Garrison, man of mystery."

"Teddy Garrison? You know Teddy Garrison?"

"He and my Pops are very close."

"The mentor that Garrison referred to in his note?"

"That'd be Pops."

I sat slack jawed with my hands still on the wheel. "Wait a minute," I said, feeling a sudden gurgle of irritation. "Why didn't you tell me that earlier?"

Edg vaulted over the convertible door. "You want to talk to him or not?"

"Yeah, I want to talk to him. But you..."

"Move it or lose it, now or never, you snooze you lose," he called back over his shoulder as he strode up the cobblestone walk.

"Wait!" I called after him. "Shouldn't we call first?"

Edg stopped at the porch and turned back to me. "Oh, well, by all means," he said with a withering British snarl. "That approach has worked famously thus far."

I couldn't argue with that, so I joined him at the front door.

I rang the bell. A dog barked. I knocked. Another bark. We waited. I shuffled my feet. I rang again. The dog obliged again. "Not home," I said, trying to conceal my relief.

"Or not answering," said Edg as he squinted through the near opaque stained glass. "Let's go around back."

To my dismay, he took off across the yard and disappeared around the side of the house. I looked around for the cops.

"Hey!" I stage-whispered after him. "What are you doing?"

I took a quick inventory of my choices: I could stand there and shuffle my feet like an idiot, I could jump back in the car and get the hell out of there, or I could swallow my paranoia and pursue Edg in his trespass.

"Oh, shit," I hissed, as I dashed across the yard and felt the little hairs on the back of my neck prickling in angst. I pushed through a thick hedge of fragrant jasmine and emerged into a lush, perfectly manicured landscape. A black wrought iron fence trimmed the perimeter of a perfect kelly green lawn. In the center of the yard stood a hardwood gazebo, and in the center of the gazebo stood Edg. He waved me over, so I walked up the steps and joined him on the platform. He looked over at the house with a slight, almost wistful, smile.

"Nice place, huh?" he said.

"Yeah. Striking. Now let's go."

"Nah. Chill out. It's okay for us to hang here a while. Nobody will mind." He leaned against the railing. "Now let's talk about that note."

By this time, I wasn't sure I believed in coincidences, but, for lack of an alternative explanation, I had slipped the note into my back pocket as we left my apartment. Registering no hint of surprise, Edg took the note from me and scanned it again like he had at my kitchen table.

"What do you make of this?" he asked.

"Well, he seems to be explaining, or justifying, his decision to leave XinoniX." I thought for a moment. "And that's really interesting, considering he didn't have to explain *anything* to me. He doesn't even know me."

"You spent a little time with my friend, Smitty, yesterday."

"Yeah... what's that got to do with it?"

"Learn anything?"

"Uh... read the signs?"

"Read the signs." He held up the note. "What does this sign say to you?"

"What do you mean?"

"I mean, what if this had nothing, ultimately, to do with Janice, Jeffers, XinoniX, or Garrison? What if it were written entirely for your benefit?"

"For my benefit? That's nuts. It makes no sense."

"Oh, well, sure. There's nothing nuts about this at all. Other than the fact that it was delivered by a *cat*," he sneered. "When did making sense become an important criterion in this bizarre little scenario of yours?"

"Touché," I said.

"Now," he said, "read the sign."

I read the note again, the romantic in me half-expecting to see it radiate with a mysterious, unearthly, sign-worthy glow. But I saw the same words, the same paper, and the same tight, normal human script.

"I'm not getting anything," I said, rubbing my thumb between my eyes. "The psychic hotline must be down again."

"Uh-huh," he said, clearly unamused. "Let's try another approach. Put it down."

I folded the note and slipped it back into my pocket.

"Garrison wrote this to you because you contacted him, right?"

I nodded.

"And you contacted Garrison because Janice asked you to find him?"

I nodded again.

"And why did she come to you in the first place?"

"Because she values me as a counselor, I guess."

"More than you do," said Edg.

"Beg your pardon?"

"It seems to me that she has a greater belief in your abilities than you do."

"That sounds familiar," I said, as I fished around for the note.

"Leave it," he said. "It's not going anywhere."

I complied.

"Think about what happened in her office the other day. What was going on with her?"

"Well," I recalled, "she was dispirited, disheartened, and ready to quit her job."

"And you helped rekindle her fire, didn't you?"

"I can't take credit for that."

"What can you take credit for?"

"I guess I just asked the right question?"

He looked at me.

"I asked the right question," I said, turning it into a statement.

"Which was?"

"Which was, 'Why do you love your job?'"

"Now, how about asking the right question for you?"

"How about you giving me a clue." I was getting impatient. I felt myself chafe, as if I were developing an emotional rash.

"Okay. Here's one. Do you know what the word *audacious* means?"

"You mean audacious as in LEAP?"

"That's the one. Audacity is a bold and blatant disregard for normal constraints. But if you look it up in *Webster's Thesaurus*, you'll see that it has a couple of connotations. One is audacity as it relates to courage, and the other is the audacity synonymous with impudence, temerity, or brazenness."

"I bet you were a lit major."

He chuckled at himself, "I try to do my homework. But the difference between the two meanings," he went on, "comes down to love versus ego. Love-inspired audacity is courageous and bold and filled with valor. It's the kind of audacity that's required to change the world for the better. Ego-inspired audacity is just a pain in the ass. In other words, some people are audacious just for the purpose of drawing attention to themselves; they're not concerned about anything other than their image."

"Is that my clue? Are you calling me a pain in the ass?" I was kidding, I hoped.

"That depends."

"On what?"

"Did you go to Janice's office out of love and compassion for her and her predicament or because it would look good on your résumé as an executive coach?"

"I didn't even think about my résumé," I said, sounding, I'm sure, as defensive as I felt. "And I'm not even getting paid for this."

"Hey," Edg laughed, "I believe you. So if love is your motivation for helping her, what are you trying to accomplish?"

"I'd like her to be happier in her job and be a better leader for her company."

Edg stepped back from the gazebo's railing, closed his eyes, stretched his arms way above his head, and let out a thunderous yawn. The dog barked inside Garrison's house. I gaped at Edg.

"I'm sorry," I scowled. "Am I keeping you from your nappy time?"

"Sorry, dude. No offense, but that's just so... normal," said Edg as he boosted himself up and sat on the gazebo's railing. He let his legs swing under him. He reminded me of a little kid sitting on a swing at the playground. "This time," he said, "I want to hear some audacity, dude! *What are you trying to accomplish?*"

"I want to help Janice reenergize her company?"

"Are you asking me or telling me? C'mon, quit screwing around."

"Okay," I gave in. "Let me give it an earnest try. What I want to accomplish, audaciously speaking, is—" I waited for the appropriate inspiring words to spring forth from my lips. Waiting for inspiring words, I've noticed, all but guarantees they won't show up.

"What?"

"I want to help Janice save the human race." I felt my cheeks flush, and I immediately started searching for a different, less embarrassing answer. It sounded too cliché, too Hallmark Card, too Successories. The problem was I meant it. Janice's mission, I realized, had struck a chord with me. I wanted a piece of her legacy. I wanted to be able to say that I played a significant role in changing the world, and not because it would look good on my résumé. Even though it would.

Edg grinned. "There you go. You want to change the world by helping to save the human race. Now, if you take that intent seriously and give it the thought it deserves, you'll think of thousands of ways you can use your talent to do it. But for now, helping Janice is a damned good place to start, it seems to me."

I noticed myself nodding in agreement, even though hesitation and doubt still showed on my face. "It still seems a little abstract to me. I don't want it to, Edg, but it does. Maybe it comes from years of conditioning in the business world. Words like *trust* and *love*, and phrases like *change the world*, even though I know they're important, are usually scoffed at and dismissed as soft."

"Who dismisses them?"

"Well, the hard-core, no-nonsense business types, mostly."

"Those days are over." Edg took off his shades and wiped them between the folds of his Tommy Bahama shirt. "The sun is setting on those so-called hard-core types. All you have to do is look at the stock market in the wake of Enron, Andersen, WorldCom, ImClone, and Tyco—remember them?—followed by the Madoff debacle, the subprime blowup, the bank bailouts, and the Wall St. meltdown. All you have to do is watch your 401(k) evaporate with your retirement dreams, and you'll see that trust and love and values are anything but touchy-feely. Now, even the average guy on the street knows that integrity and his bank account are intimately connected. Trust and love and humanity *are* hard-core business principles. The posers have been exposed; the Extreme Leaders are going to emerge.

"This will be the age of love-inspired audacity," he continued, picking up a full head of steam. "Now is the time for all of us to take our power back and become, each of us, Extreme Leaders in our own right. We have to set a new example of what's right in business and everywhere else. We have to be audacious enough to follow the examples we respect and challenge the ones we don't.

"An underling who shreds suspect documents because the boss told her to do it is choosing to be just that, an underling. That person is making a conscious choice to perpetuate rotten leadership and is, therefore, a party to it.

"But if that underling looks into her own heart, finds the values that reside there and summons the audacity to do what's right and honorable, she chooses to reject the boss's order and take the consequences, she has then stepped into the role of Extreme Leader, and by her stance contributes to the creation of a better world. I wonder what would have happened at Andersen if more of their consultants had made that choice."

"Wait a minute," I said. "Andersen had great people; I know a lot of them personally. They lost their jobs because of a few idiots at the top. It's not fair to put the blame on the accountants and office workers."

"Okay. Maybe the outcome for Andersen wouldn't have changed. We'll never know. But I do know this. it's very easy to sit back and point the accusing finger at a few number perverse thugs at the top. Very easy. We're all doing a lot of finger-pointing these days, and even though a few bad guys are going to the slammer, that doesn't solve much in our own lives."

"All right, Edg," I said, "I hear you. But let's say you're talking to your average, everyday corporate employee or supervisor. Or manager. What will you say to them?"

"Average is a pejorative."

"You know what I mean."

"I'd tell them the same thing I'm telling you, make a commitment, right now, that no matter where you sit on the org chart, no matter what it says in your job description, stand up for what's right and normal constraints be damned.

"The world needs you right now. The world needs your influence and your audacious action. Your actions will require you to find strength in your heart. Never let anyone tell you that your heart's not big enough, and don't believe the hype that the world is controlled by a select few. Nobody controls your world unless you choose to let them.

"Take a stand; put your skin in the game; advocate for integrity. This is the time to shift the image, behavior, and, ultimately, the legacy of business, and you do that through your own behavior and example.

"You may not think you can change the Whole World that we live in—and you may be wrong—but you can certainly change the world—small *w*—that you and yours live in: the world of your company, the world of your employees, the world of your industry, or the world of your family. To deny that is to deny your capability as a human being.

"But, hey... it's your choice."

Just then I heard a phone ring inside the house. The answering machine clicked on, and a familiar message drifted through an open window on the second floor and, it seemed, spoke to me through the breeze: "*Who are you and what do you want?*" A bead of sweat rolled down my back. The caller hung up.

Edg was grinning; I wasn't.

■ TWENTY-ONE

Bob Jeffers was in the hospital. He had collapsed at the office on Saturday at the same time, it turns out, that Edg was grilling me at Garrison's gazebo. At first they thought it was a heart attack, but it proved to be some kind of stress-related panic attack. Janice had ridden with him to the hospital, which was only fair because she was the one who had flattened him.

Saturday at XinoniX is a peaceful time. A few people with pressing deadlines will show up in their shorts and flip-flops to work without the distractions of a typical weekday. This Saturday, however, the office was empty. At least Janice thought it was. Bob Jeffers thought so too. They worked in their own self-contained offices, absorbed in their tasks, each blissfully unaware of the other, when Mama Nature, in her infinite humor, set off their biological pagers at precisely the same moment.

Janice put down her pen. Jeffers pushed away from his computer. Janice stepped into her hallway. Jeffers pulled his door shut and locked it. Janice turned right, Jeffers, left. They sprinted toward the bathroom, rounded the blind corner from opposite directions, and smacked right into each other.

The shock was too much for Bob: he clutched his chest and fell over backwards, cracking his head on the wall on the way down. A less honorable person in Janice's shoes might have seen the situation as an opportunity to let her corporate adversary expire before her eyes, strains of "Ding-dong! The Witch is Dead" chiming cheerily in her head. But Janice lunged for the nearest phone and called 911. Then she rode in the ambulance and, I've been told, held the 51% Guy's hand all the way to the hospital.

Adversity, someone once said, doesn't build character; it reveals it.

We had been camped in Garrison's backyard for so long that I was beginning to feel at home on that gazebo. That was odd, considering I hadn't met our host.

As usual, Edg had given me a lot to think about, and I was feeling emotionally provoked, intellectually stimulated, and physically exhausted. My cell phone chirped and I apologized to Edg as I answered. Janice filled me in on the scene at the hospital and on the events that had brought her there. Edg listened in on my end of the conversation.

"You're where? What happened? Really? You're kidding. Is he all right? Why do you want me there? Well, sure, I suppose I could come if that's what you really want. I'll be there as soon as I can." I rang off and looked at Edg.

"Garrison and I will have to meet some other day," I said. "Duty calls. I have to go to the hospital."

"Everything okay?" he asked.

"Seems so. That was Janice, she's in the hospital with Bob Jeffers." I gave him the quick sketch. "She says she wants to have a heart-to-heart with him right now."

"Sounds like your opportunity," he said, pushing his small, dark shades up the bridge of his nose.

"For what?"

"That's for you to know and you to find out."

I didn't have the time, energy, or patience to pursue that one.

Edg told me that he was going to hang around for a while, and, over my protests, he convinced me to go directly to the hospital.

"Don't worry about me," he said. "I'll find my way home."

As I cut back through the hedge and around the side of the house, the dog barked again, and, to my surprise, I heard the back door open and shut.

I turned around and sprinted back to the yard. Edg was gone.

"Sonofabitch," I said to myself. "Garrison was in there the whole time."

As I opened the door to the Mustang, I happened to glance back at the house, and for a moment it seemed that the house was looking back at me. But it wasn't the house; it was two pairs of eyes in the upstairs window, one belonging to a little brown kitty cat, and the other to a dog. A retriever. And it sure as hell looked a lot like Sadie.

■ TWENTY-TWO

I was anxious. It was visiting hours at Sharp Hospital, so getting into Jeffers's room wouldn't be a problem. I had no idea what to expect once I did, though. Janice was counting on me for something. To facilitate, she'd said. That's one of those loaded words that means different things to different people. I knew some facilitators who would be showing up right now with a box of mango-scented markers and a pad of flip-chart paper. I didn't think that's what Janice had in mind.

I had no pens or paper, but I had other advantages: (1) I had worked with Jeffers before, and, as far as I could tell, he liked me well enough. (2) I had, it goes without saying, a great relationship with Janice, and, for some reason, she trusted me. And (3)—this was the big one—I wanted to help Jeffers, Janice, and XinoniX save the world.

I don't know if I was romanticizing or blowing this way out of proportion, but it suddenly occurred to me that the stakes were enormous. And right then, with my hand resting on the door handle as I hesitated in the hallway outside of Jeffers's room, I felt as though some significant piece of the future would be determined in the next few minutes. The livelihood, and perhaps lives, of a lot of people were unknowingly dependent on the outcome of the imminent conversation. XinoniX's future would depend on both Janice and Jeffers staying there, and staying there to work together. And their staying there would somehow depend on me.

And right then, in that moment, two words came to mind.

Janice was sitting in a chair in a corner of the otherwise vacant room. The bed was empty, and there was no sign of Jeffers as she stood up to greet me. She was wearing shorts and a tank top, Saturday work clothes, and her red eyes were a sharp contrast to the pallor of her face. Janice looked whipped.

"Is he dead?" I asked, trying in my own perverted way to lighten the mood with a bit of gallows humor.

"That's not funny," said Janice with a scowl. "For a minute I thought I'd killed him, and believe me, there wasn't an ounce of humor in the situation. Turns out it was just some kind of panic attack, that and a pretty good bump on the head, but it scared the living hell out of me."

"Sorry," I said. "I'm a little uneasy myself, I guess. So where is he?"

"Bathroom."

"Think he made it this time?"

Janice laughed in spite of herself. Gallows humor sometimes misses the mark, but relentless gallows humor will eventually nail the bull's-eye.

"So, what's the plan?" I asked.

"Basically, I just wanted you here for moral support, to hold my hand, emotionally speaking, while I do what I have to do."

"Which is what?"

"Resign."

"Oh shit," I started to say, but I didn't get the chance, because just then the door swung open and an orderly wheeled Bob Jeffers into the room.

Janice may have looked bad, but next to Jeffers she was fresh as a springtime daisy. His skin was gray, and his thick salt-and-pepper hair was sticking up from behind a gauze bandage. Stocky white legs jutted out from under the hospital-issue gown, and his feet were tucked into black calf-length GoldToe socks. His legendary 51% blowhard bravado had run up against his own mortality and nearly been overruled. When he saw me, his eyes sparked with quizzical recognition.

"Steve Farber, right? It's been a long time."

"Hi Bob," I said, extending my hand into empty space. "How are you feeling?"

He glanced at Janice, then back at me, and took my floating hand in his surprisingly strong grasp.

"Lucky. I'm feeling lucky. New lease on life and all that," he sighed. "But, and I don't mean to be impolite, what are you doing here?"

"I asked him to come," said Janice before I could reply. "If you're feeling up to it, I thought the three of us could talk."

The orderly helped Jeffers back onto the bed, said "15 minutes left of visiting hours," and slipped out of the room. We looked at each other in uncomfortable silence. Janice and I sat, and Jeffers picked up a paper cup and munched thoughtfully on a mouthful of shaved ice.

"We know you need to rest," I said to Jeffers. "So if you'd rather do this later, I'd certainly understand." I was hoping, frankly, for a response that would liberate me fom this place. I never liked hospitals. Or conflict. Conflict in a hospital was a double whammy that I was sure I could live without.

He swallowed and said, "I don't know what you want to talk about, but I suppose I can take anything for 14 minutes."

But who's counting?

Janice cleared her throat conspicuously, and we both looked over to her. *Here we go*, I thought.

"Bob," she began. "I think it's time for me to..."

"Put things on the table," I butted in. "That's why she asked me here. To see if I could help you guys sort things out." I knew it wasn't polite to talk over another person, at least that's what they taught in facilitator school, but sometimes the end did justify the means. I barged ahead before Janice could recover from the shock of my intrusion. Only 13 minutes left. No time for subtlety. I took a deep breath.

"Bob," I said, "do you know that everyone at your company thinks you're a jerk?" I heard Janice gasp. "Your employees and executives, including Janice, think you're an autocratic, uncaring, out of touch bureaucrat who doesn't give a rat's ass about the future of XinoniX."

He stopped chomping on his ice. No turning back now, I thought.

"But," I said, before he could get a word in, "I have it on good authority—Garrison, as a matter of fact—that it's not true." I shot a looked at an addled Janice. "It's an unfortunate misperception of who you really are and what you really want."

Now both of their mouths were hanging open. Mine kept moving.

I turned to Janice. "Let me tell you what Garrison says. He says that Bob is a brilliant strategist. He says that Bob's abilities to analyze and execute are second to none and that XinoniX would have no future without him."

"When did you find Teddy?" gasped Janice.

I ignored the question. "But you already know that, don't you, Bob?"

He looked at the floor, hesitated, and said, "Yes."

Janice trembled with anger. But before she could call him an arrogant prick or something less flowery, I forged on. "But you also know something else, right?"

"Yes," he said. "Yes, I do."

"What?" shouted Janice.

He turned his head and, for the first time that I'd noticed, looked her in the eye. He said, "I suck at the people thing. But you're a superstar in that department. I can't do this without you, without your influence."

Her jaw dropped again, and I saw in her eyes that she was frantically trying to process this new information.

"Listen," he said. "I know that what Steve says is true. I've tried hard to deny it, I admit, but this experience," he waved his hand around to indicate his hospital room, "has been a wake-up call, to borrow a phrase."

"How so?" I asked.

"I'm stressed out. I'm not sure that I can live up to everyone's expectations of me. When I took over for Garrison I knew I was stepping into a business that he built, in large part, with his personality and charisma." He paused, sighed again. "Not my strong suits. Don't get me wrong, I'm a good businessman. I've got a successful track record. I'm proud of what I've done in my life, but Teddy's a tough act to follow. People not only respect him, they love him. From what you've told me, and, like I said, I already know it, I'm not scoring very high on either of those measures."

"Do you regret taking the job?" I asked, surprised by his candor.

He looked around the room. "Remains to be seen. I regret that something about it made me end up here, that's for sure."

"Why'd you take the job in the first place?"

"The rumor is that the board hired me and forced Teddy out, but that's not true. He recruited me. He told me the XinoniX story, laid out the vision and the challenges, and appealed to what he called my unequaled business acumen. That was a nice compliment, but that's not why I signed up."

Janice was mute. I asked, "Why did you?"

"I saw it as my opportunity to do something significant for the world."

I felt my skin tingle. "Do what for the world?"

He hesitated, looked down at his hands. "Save it," he whispered.

"Meaning?"

Another hesitation. "Well... this may sound strange coming from me, but I've come to appreciate that there's more to business than numbers. Yes, numbers are important, to say the least, and I'm a master when it comes to that. And there's no doubt that when the numbers are good we get paid accordingly. I've hit my share of numbers in my life, and I've been rewarded well for doing it. But I've had this growing, persistent feeling that something vital's been missing."

"Like what?" asked Janice.

"I've had a hard time putting it into words. Soul? Meaning? Impact? Don't know, exactly." He looked my way. "I once heard your pal, Tom Peters, say that his nightmare is to have his tombstone read, 'He made budget.' I can relate to that. I want my legacy to mean something. So I joined XinoniX to do something important, and I figured that if I could do that, the numbers would follow."

"So, what do you want on your tombstone, Bob?" I asked with a wry allusion to the pizza commercial.

"He *helped.*"

Janice looked stunned. "Why didn't you ever say this to me, Bob?"

"Never said it to anybody."

"Why not?"

Bob shrugged.

"Bob?" said Janice.

"Yeah?"

"You suck at the people thing."

Bob's shoulders shook, and I heard a sound that I'd never heard from him before. He was laughing.

"That's what I need you for, Janice. Would you help me with that?"

She looked up at the ceiling and drew in a deep breath. "Sign me up," she said.

"Okay," I said, getting up out of my chair. "Seems like the two of you have a common agenda after all. Aren't you glad we had this little chat?" It was a question that required no answer.

"Now there's something else you guys gotta do."

"What?" they asked in unison.

"Prove you mean it."

Sunday

■ TWENTY-THREE

Janice was on her way to my apartment. I had promised her an explanation about Garrison as we'd stood in the hospital parking lot after yesterday's encounter. I'd put her off, invoking fatigue and near brain death.

I had stopped at the supermarket on the way home and bought myself a Saturday night recuperation kit: a liter of Diet Coke, a frozen pizza—guess which kind—a container of Ben and Jerry's Cherry Garcia, and a tub of Cool Whip. One of the cable stations was running a *Twilight Zone* marathon which, for some reason, seemed appropriate.

So now, on this bright Sunday morning, I drank my coffee and nursed an all-out sugar and fat hangover, while I tried to collect my thoughts and achieve enough brainwave coherence to explain to Janice my sort of encounter with Garrison. I wasn't having much success.

I read the Sunday comics and found myself pining for a new *Far Side* cartoon. Gary Larson's cows always had a way of putting things in perspective. I thought of the one where a man-cow was sitting in his easy chair reading the paper.

His wife-cow wore a designer dress and dangly earrings and held a glass of wine in her hoof. She gazed wistfully out the window of their beautiful, palatial home and said, "Wendell, I'm not content."

I often think of that cartoon. Must be a sign.

I stepped out on the balcony and looked down on the street just as Janice pulled into a parking space across the way. As she stepped out of her Pathfinder, I happened to glance up the street to my left and saw Edg coming toward her on his skateboard. He saw Janice and screeched to a halt, flipping his board up and grabbing it in his hand. He didn't seem to panic, exactly, but he looked around as if trying to calculate an escape route. He jumped back on his board and took off to his right down the alley behind the neighboring apartment building. Gone. Edg didn't strike me as the type to engage in wimpy avoidance behavior, but it sure looked like that's what he'd just done.

Janice, oblivious to the scene, slipped her keys into her purse and crossed the street toward me. "Hey!" she called up to me. "Can I come up?"

We sat on a couple of tall stools that I had strategically positioned on the balcony to afford a view of the sparkling bay. A soft breeze rustled the fronds of my old friend, Mr. Palm. Another perfect San Diego Sunday, that is, except for my dull sugar headache.

"Okay," she said, "dish."

I produced the note and handed it to her, figuring that that would communicate the essence of the situation. I had neither the desire nor the energy to spell out the whole scenario in detail.

"A note straight from the horse's mouth," I said, mixing a metaphor like others would a martini.

She scrunched up her eyebrows as her gaze zigzagged through the script. "I don't understand that man. Why wouldn't he just call and talk to me about this?"

"Seemed pretty clear to me," I said. "He wants you to grow without his help. Consider yourself weaned from the leadership teat of Teddy Garrison." God, I love metaphors.

"Okay, but he..."

"Forget about him for the time being, Janice. Garrison helped to get you this far but you're the one who has to make the leap, you know?"

"What if I can't?"

"Well, here's what my friend, Edg, would tell you."

"Who?"

"That's a whole other story for another time. Anyway, he'd say that your love for XinoniX, its products, and its people will give you the energy to be audacious, bold, and courageous. If you keep reminding yourself and others about the importance of your work, about the great future you're striving to create, you'll generate the energy you need to work through any obstacle and challenge. Your energy will be contagious to others, including Jeffers, just as Garrison's was to you.

"I saw your lights go on, Janice. I saw it the other morning in your office, I saw it yesterday at the hospital, and I see it now. Love generates energy. That's the simple truth. You already know it, consciously or not. You may think you're still vacillating on your leadership role, but your heart has already committed to the cause."

"You sound pretty sure about that."

"I am."

"How can you be more convinced about me than I am?"

"Doesn't have to be that way. You're just missing one last step."

"Which is?"

"Love requires proof. You have to prove it to yourself and you have to prove it to everyone around you."

"How?"

"Let's start with *when*."

"Okay, then, when?"

I had already given this a lot of thought. "Is Jeffers going to work tomorrow?"

"So he told me."

"Are you? Because that would be a requirement in this whole leadership thing."

"Ha-ha. Yes, I'm going to work. You heard me promise Bob that I'd stay."

"Okay. Tomorrow, then. Let's give XinoniX a reason to celebrate the coming of Monday."

"That'd be a switch," she said.

"Well... you need a switch to turn on the lights." Now that was a good metaphor, straight from the horse's teat.

We spent the next couple of hours putting our plan together, and by the time we'd finished, both Janice and

I felt that Monday had the potential to be the start of not only a new week, but also of a new, re-energized XinoniX.

As afternoon tilted toward evening, Janice headed off to brief Jeffers on his role in Monday's events and to make sure he was on board. I pulled on a sweatshirt and headed out for a stroll; it was all up to them now.

I paused at the end of the walkway and looked up at my old friend, Mr. Palm. For the first time in a long while, I didn't feel the need for a smack on the head to get me to think clearly. I was feeling pretty good about my new perspective on my life and my work.

I had always liked it when people asked me what I did for work, and I answered proudly with labels like *leadership coach, consultant, seminar leader,* or *speaker.* It was different, even glamorous, and always made for interesting and lively conversation. But what had dawned on me with increasing brilliance over the past few days was the disturbing realization that the roles I played were fundamentally empty and nearly devoid of meaning. It all sounded great, but I hadn't really strived to do anything of lasting significance. I had been working with leaders, but I hadn't been leading. I had spoken with conviction, but I hadn't been convinced. I had inspired a few people to action, but I hadn't, when I looked at my work with cold, objective scrutiny, done diddly do.

It was different now. Fundamentally altered. I was falling in love with my job or, more accurately, I was quitting my job and taking up a calling. Not that I was anything special, not by any measure, but I was, at last, crystal-clear about what I wanted to accomplish in my time on this planet. And when I thought about this newfound mission to change whatever part of the world I touched, I felt a real, authentic, warmth stirring in my heart. Love, to put it simply.

As I allowed myself the indulgence of this wonderful feeling, I noticed that I really didn't care if my thoughts sounded like the text of a Hallmark card. From this day forward, I vowed to myself as I stood there under the tree, with every bit of energy and audacity I could muster I would approach my life and every client engagement with the expressed intent of transforming the world. And if I fell short of the mark or even failed completely, I wouldn't have the slightest residue of regret because my intent would always be noble. I was leaping, damn it. And it was exhilarating.

Even though I had been working a long time in the leadership arena, my encounter with Janice, Jeffers, and XinoniX felt like a beginning. Would they turn things around over there? I didn't know. Would Janice be a considerably better leader as a result of the effort? Most assuredly so. I had no doubt that she would go on to do astoundingly great things, regardless of what would, or wouldn't, happen tomorrow. And that felt... well, totally awesome, dude.

As I got ready for bed that evening, it occurred to me that aside from the odd, distant glimpse from my balcony, I hadn't seen Edg since I'd left him Saturday afternoon on Garrison's gazebo. I really liked the guy, so I'm not embarrassed to admit that I kind of missed him. Our conversations had had a remarkable effect on the way I was thinking about the world and my place in it. And in our very brief time together, I had fallen into a deep well of gratitude for him and his insights. He'd asked for nothing in return yet, for some reason, I'd never questioned his motives. At our second meeting, he had said that I'd be doing him a great favor, but I'd seen no evidence of that. Maybe he'd just wanted someone to pick on.

I flicked on the TV and tuned in to the local evening news in time to see the weather forecast. In San Diego, there's not much drama in the climate story. The coastal temperature highs and lows average 70 or so; tack on another 10 to 20 degrees, and there's your inland temperature. That's the whole story.

In other words, the weather report didn't demand a lot of focus, so I almost missed the story that came next. The name, William Maritime, snapped my attention back to the TV like a bungee cord on a bridge jumper.

The anchor was saying, "The reclusive multimillionaire and philanthropist died late this afternoon at San Diego Memorial Hospital. The cause of death has not been confirmed, but sources close to the late Mr. Maritime tell us that he had been battling cancer for some time. He had spent his final days quietly in a mobile home in North County, San Diego. Here's Jennifer Lee with a retrospective on the widely loved, deeply respected, and some would say, mysterious businessman."

I sat on the edge of my bed, as my heart fell to my stomach and flopped around as though it were drowning in there. No wonder I hadn't seen Edg today.

"Oh man," I said out loud. "Oh man, oh man, oh man."

I had no way to reach Edg. I had no idea where he lived; and I had a crushing fear that I wouldn't see him again for a long time.

I fished around in my pocket for the note that Pops had given me just a couple of days, it seemed like eons, earlier. I held in my hands the only tangible evidence that I had, in fact, spent a few miraculous hours with the great man and that he, justified or not, had decided to believe in me. Now he was gone. The written word always outlasts the man.

This note, I knew, would be the fuel I would run on for the rest of my life. It had taken Pops a few minutes to write it; it would power me forever. I read it over and over until the words were etched in my brain and, certainly, on my heart. I closed my eyes and watched the words fall and float in the darkness behind my eyelids. My heart stopped.

Frantic, I pulled Garrison's note from the other pocket of my jean shorts and held the two scripts side by side. And then everything fell into place with a resounding click.

Monday

■ TWENTY-FOUR

Monday morning at XinoniX started earlier than usual for Janice and Jeffers. They had met in the office at 6:30 and polished the agenda for the companywide meeting, which had been called for 10:00. I arrived at 9:00, got my visitor's pass, and waited for the two of them in the executive conference room.

I hadn't heard from Edg, and I found it hard to think of anything else, so I did what I normally do when I'm feeling agitated and distracted: I paced. My eyes wandered along the conference room walls. They provided a kind of visual history of the company. On one wall was a gallery of framed XinoniX marketing brochures and articles from the *Wall Street Journal, Barron's, Fortune, Forbes,* and several other business publications. On the other was picture after picture of the XinoniX gang from various parties and company events. The biggest and most conspicuous picture was a group shot with a caption that read, *All of Us.* Because I'd never seen a picture of Garrison, I wanted to try and pick him out in the crowd. But before I could get close enough to see the photo clearly, Janice and Bob came through the door.

They looked good, and I heard something approaching nervous cheer in their voices as they bid me good morning. Bob was wearing khaki pants and a soft, black sport coat over a white silk tee shirt, his head bandage replaced by an oversized Band-Aid. Janice wore a XinoniX logo polo shirt tucked into her usual crisp-pressed designer jeans. I was glad I had opted for the casual look myself, mainly because I had woken up too late and been far too tired to wrestle with a necktie.

"Showtime," said Janice as she beckoned me to the door.

The XinoniX crowd was already gathering in the cafeteria when we made our entrance. I helped myself to a cup of coffee and a bagel as Bob and Janice circulated through the room, shaking hands and making small talk.

As I stood at the table and dumped creamer and Equal in my cup, I overheard a couple of people (I always learn a lot when I'm anonymous) offering each other their take on the upcoming proceedings.

"This should be interesting," said the guy with the cranberry muffin. "I don't think I've heard Jeffers say a single word since he's been here."

"Yeah, *interesting*," said the woman with the fruit plate. "I've seen this kind of crap a hundred times. The last thing I need is a bunch of rah rah crap. At my last company, we had a town hall meeting every week. It was always empty condescending crap. I have too much crap to do to spend my time listening to a bunch of crap from people who don't really give a crap about me."

"Yeah," said Muffin Man. "I hear ya."

I took a sip of my coffee, and for some reason it tasted like crap.

I sat at the back of the room so I could get the widest possible perspective of the group. I sipped and munched while the cafeteria filled up. Janice stepped to the front and thumped the microphone.

"Can you hear me okay?"

I nodded my head vigorously, put down my cup, and gave her an enthusiastic thumbs-up.

"Please have a seat and we'll get started in a few minutes."

"Oh, hooray," someone muttered.

I looked to my left. It was Crap Lady, sitting right next to me. What a great opportunity for an attitudinal experiment.

"Excuse me," I said. "I was thinking about getting some fruit. How is it?"

"Not too bad," she said through a mouthful. "But this is California; kinda hard to screw up fruit in California."

I had a feeling that was high praise, coming from her.

"This coffee tastes like crap," I offered.

"Always does," she said.

Surprise, surprise, I thought.

The murmuring in the cafeteria subsided as Jeffers took a seat facing the crowd and Janice returned to the mic.

"Good morning!" she enthused.

The group mumbled a response.

"Is it still morning?" queried my neighbor under her breath.

"Let's try that again, good morning!"

Another collective mumble.

Oh, boy, I thought, *tough room.*

I scanned the crowd one more time and then focused my full attention on Janice. I think I was more nervous than she was. Totally unfounded, as it turned out.

She began, "Before I give the microphone to Bob, I just want to take a few minutes to tell you why we're here." She paused. "No... let me tell you why *I'm here*. And, frankly, I almost wasn't.

"I joined this company because I believed in what we had, and I believed in what we had because Teddy Garrison painted such a compelling, awesome picture of the future. And in a very short time, his vision infected and inspired me, and I found myself not only believing in XinoniX, but also falling in love with it."

She looked around the room and, it seemed to me, made eye contact with all 300 people.

"I would wake up every morning and literally jump out of bed. In fact, there were many nights I didn't go to bed at all. Nobody ever made me stay up all night to meet an important client deadline. Nobody ever made me feel like I'd be a slacker if I didn't push myself. The only person I ever had to answer to was myself. And although there were many times that I was really, really tired, I was never exhausted.

"Just out of curiosity," she said, scanning the crowd, "how many of you can remember feeling the same way?"

At least 80% of the hands went up, including my neighbor's.

"That's what I thought. And be honest, please. How many of you still feel that way?"

After a lot of shuffling and sidelong glances, four hands went up—reluctantly, it seemed.

"I, for one, thank goodness for the four of you, because as you may have noticed I did not raise my hand. And I'm supposed to be a leader. I've been thinking about this a lot, trying to figure out what went wrong for me."

She paused and looked down at her hands.

"I was really pissed off when Teddy left. I felt abandoned and betrayed by the very person whose vision I had taken as my own. I couldn't believe that everything we had worked for was so *meaningless* to him that he could discard us like a sack of trash. That's what it felt like to me. Was I the only one?"

Several shaking heads, many murmurs of no.

"It looks as though I'm speaking for many of you. And that may be true. But let me speak only for myself for a moment when I say that I've been a complete idiot. Not an idiot for believing in XinoniX, but for tying that belief to one person.

"Teddy was a great leader for us. No doubt. But he was not the be-all and end-all; he was not the ultimate factor in our success. In fact, that's exactly why he was a great leader, he built a company that could succeed without him; not because of him. When I realized that, it suddenly became clear exactly what had gone wrong for me. I'd forgotten one vital thing: This is *our* company, dammit."

Her face flushed.

"The people in this room developed and continue to develop our exceptional software, the people in this room sell that exceptional software, the people in this room take superb care of our clients, the people in this room—every one of us—can change the world if we want to. And I want to.

"Rumors have been circulating that I'm leaving XinoniX. Last week those rumors may have been true. But I'm here to tell you that I'm not going to leave. And I'm not going to stay only to go through the motions, collect a paycheck, and live my life on the weekends. As of today, right now, I recommit myself to our success and to the success of our clients. My energy is back, and I won't let it wane again. And, quite frankly, whether or not you choose to come along with me, I'm charging ahead. But I want you to come with me.

"Some of you may be thinking that, as an executive, I'm supposed to talk like this whether I mean it or not. Others of you may suspect that I'm making a calculated attempt to pump you up; to motivate the troops in a desperate last-ditch effort to save XinoniX. I might feel the same way if the roles were reversed.

"I'm not trying to change your hearts and minds; it's been challenging enough to change my own. All I can tell you is that I love this place and I love what we can become, and I am completely, unabashedly, and unapologetically in love with the kind of future we can create together."

The room was electric; I could tell she was getting through, and I damn near stood up and applauded. I opted for professional constraint.

Janice said, "I'm asking each of you to do only one thing for now. Ask yourself the same question I asked myself: Why did you love XinoniX before, and how can you get that feeling back? If you can, then let's get about the business of making our distinct mark on the world. If you can't, then ask for help. I had to. I got my help from a close friend and confidant—"

Now my face flushed.

"... and from Bob Jeffers." She looked over at Jeffers, and he appeared genuinely surprised at Janice's comment.

"And if you can't get that feeling back, and if you don't want to ask for help, then—and this is just the simple truth—it's time for you to leave and find your passion somewhere else. Life's too short; don't live it without your heart."

She stopped and let silence fill the room. Janice Everson had just revealed herself to her colleagues and done it magnificently. I knew there wasn't one single ounce of bullshit in that entire speech, but I wondered if the authenticity was as evident to the company as it was to me.

A hand went up. "Janice?"

"Yes, Sondra?"

"Was that an ultimatum?"

"Yes. Yes, I guess it was."

The room murmured.

"But it's exactly the same ultimatum I gave myself."

"Fair enough," said Sondra.

That was pretty good evidence that Janice had connected. Sondra was in. Sondra, who only minutes before had been known to me as Crap Lady.

■ TWENTY-FIVE

After a brief and sincere introduction from Janice, Bob Jeffers stepped up to the microphone. Whereas Janice had been confident and comfortable, Jeffers appeared awkward and even a little bit shy.

"I'm a little nervous," said Bob quietly into the microphone. "I think I have a reputation as a man of few words. It's not that I have nothing to say, or that I'm antisocial. Well, not entirely antisocial."

That brought a few tentative chuckles from the crowd.

"It's just that I'm, well, more of a numbers guy than a words guy. So I hope you'll be patient with me as I try to, um, express myself to you. I do have something important that I'd like to say."

He cleared his throat.

"I'd like to say that I'm sorry. And I'm asking all of you to accept my apology."

After a short, awkward silence, someone from the middle of the room called, "What are we forgiving you for, Bob?" A few more tentative giggles followed.

"I appreciate that, but I think you already know.

"Look," Bob went on, "I may be a man of few words, but I do have ears. And I hear what people say about me. Nobody here has ever called me the 51% Guy to my face, but I have heard the name, and, believe it or not, I know where it came from. The infamous 51% rule has been following me around for the past 10 years. For those of you who may never have heard about it before now, let's just say that it comes from my reputation as a boss who believes he has all the answers and has to have the final say on everything. In other words, I always have to own 51% of the vote. I always have to have it my way. Command and control. Theory X management. Right? Does that describe my reputation fairly well?"

Some people actually had the guts to nod in response to that. I was impressed, given that Bob hadn't denied it was true.

"Well... it's all true. At least it *was* true. Through most of my career, I've seen myself as the big boss, the one with all the answers, and I was never really interested in other people's, especially my *subordinates'*, ideas or opinions. If you worked for me, your input was useless. Unless, of course, it agreed with mine.

"Then, a few years ago, I had a pretty severe heart attack. Almost died. Instead of losing my life I was, thankfully, given the chance at a new one. That's when I realized that my whole approach to work and life had been unhealthy. It's unhealthy for me to act as though I have to control everything because I can't. Right? So I tried to do things differently. Tried to be more of a team player. I tried to be more inclusive. I tried that for about two weeks before I said, 'Screw it. Command and control *works* for me.'

"Then I met Teddy, and he invited me to XinoniX, but on the condition that I change my management style."

This was news to me. From the look on Janice's face, to her as well.

"A condition that I accepted and then readily ignored. And that," he glanced at the fellow in the middle of the room, "is what I'm asking your forgiveness for. Janice made a commitment to you; I will as well."

For the first time since the meeting started, he looked over to me and ever so slightly raised his eyebrows as if to say, *Okay, here goes. OS!M time!*

"I am going to be more inclusive as a manager and more supportive as a colleague to each of you in this company. I am going to do my part to help us change the world. That's an audacious intent, but I believe that all of you—our team, our company—are capable of living up to it. And I want to be a leader worthy of the task and worthy of you.

"I don't expect all of you to believe me just because I'm saying these words. I still need to prove it to you and, over time, I will. So I'm asking that we start with a clean slate. That we start over. I'm not saying that we'll run XinoniX as a democracy, or that we'll all vote on every decision. That's no way to run a business either. I'm not saying that every decision I do make will be popular. I am saying that the 51% rule is hereby abolished. And I am going to spend more time with all of you to hear your ideas and to understand your perspectives. Most important, I'm asking you to make your own decisions in your own areas of responsibility. You know what it takes to do a great job around here. I trust you to do it.

"Oh, and one more thing." He stepped away from the microphone and fumbled around in his briefcase, while Janice watched with curiosity. This, obviously, hadn't been planned.

He pulled out a lime green folder and handed it to Janice.

"I think this is yours," he said.

It was her marketing plan.

■ T W E N T Y – S I X

With the top down in the Mustang, I drove away from XinoniX and headed for home, my mind lost in what I'd just witnessed. I marveled at how, in just a few minutes, the mood of an entire company had shifted toward the north. People had stayed in the cafeteria long after the meeting adjourned talking to each other and lining up to offer their congratulations and support to Janice and Bob. They had both publicly pursued very personal OS!Ms. Now all they had to do was follow up on their commitments and continue to prove their words through their actions. I knew they would.

I don't know how it happened exactly, but I soon found myself pulling the car up to the curb in front of Pops's trailer. I noticed the roses had been recently trimmed and petals scattered on the doorstep. Probably just the wind's doing, I thought. I walked up to the door, picked up a scarlet petal, and gazed at it as it fluttered gently in the palm of my hand. For some reason, I thought about Smitty and realized that this moment was rife with significance. I was lost in a reverie of rich symbolism when the door swung slowly open.

In spite of myself, I ran through the doorway and gave the freaking brat a mighty bear hug.

"I'm... I'm... so sorry for your loss," I stammered. I've always been lousy at the grief thing; I've never known what to say to those left behind.

"It's okay, dude," he said quietly. "C'mon in."

Boxes were scattered around the trailer in various stages of being packed and taped. We walked out to the yard and sat in the same chairs we'd shared with Pops only a few days earlier. Sunshine sparkled down through the jasmine and cast speckled shadows on the porch.

"We've known for quite a while that it was coming," said Edg. "We just didn't know exactly when."

"But he looked so vibrant," I said. "I never would have guessed there was anything wrong with him."

"That's probably because he was ready to go; he'd come to terms with it. What you saw was a man deeply at peace with what he'd done with his time on this planet."

Edg took a deep breath that quavered slightly and caught momentarily in his throat. "I miss him like you wouldn't believe," he said. "And it's only been a day."

"Of course I believe it," I said. "He was your Pops." I decided not to pry about funeral or memorial arrangements;

for some reason, it didn't seem appropriate. "What about your mother?" I asked instead.

"She died shortly after I was born."

"I'm sorry," I said, flustered.

"Not your fault. Besides, Pops more than took up the slack. I never lacked for love and guidance."

"Any brothers or sisters?"

"Nope. Just me and the old man."

We sat in silence for a few moments until Edg abruptly switched gears. "I'm glad you stopped by before I left."

"What do you mean?" I asked, trying to sound calm. "Left for where?"

He laughed, which oddly didn't seem at all inappropriate, even under these circumstances. "I'm gonna take care of Pops's stuff, make a few of the necessary arrangements, and then I'm outta here. I need to get away for a while. It's time for a long overdue surfing excursion. Big waves await me at other shores."

"Wait a minute," I said. "I feel like we've just gotten started." That sounded grossly selfish, I knew, but I didn't care. It felt like a great and valuable friend was about to slip away from me, so I launched into a quick description of what had just gone down at XinoniX. I told him how he had inspired me and how I had been able to use his insight to help Janice and Bob.

"XinoniX already feels like a new company," I said. "But I know there's so much more to do. Don't bail on me now, Edg," I pleaded. "I mean, we've only scratched the surface of LEAP, right?" I noticed myself getting desperate, and I didn't like the feeling.

He answered me with a broad, classic Edg grin.

"Wait here," he said. "I've got something for you."

He jumped up and bolted into the trailer. I leaned back in my chair and stared up into the deep blue San Diego sky. An enormous pelican coasted overhead toward the ocean.

"Hey!" he said, snapping me out of my trance. "I want you to have this." He slapped a small, glossy notebook down on the bistro table. I looked at the cover. It had a pale blue background with bold black letters that said,

> A Daily Handbook for Extreme Leaders: How to Do What You Love in the Service of People Who Love What You Do
> By William G. Maritime and Son

"With this," he said, "I'm sure you can take it from here."

"You and Pops wrote this together?" I asked.

"More like we lived it together. We just did our best to capture the essence of Pops's approach to life and work. Tried to make it real simple."

"Did you publish it? I've never heard of it before," I said as I reached to pick it up.

He smiled. "That's the only copy."

I jerked my hand back as though I suddenly noticed a rattlesnake on the table. "Whoa! I can't keep this. This is yours, Edg. You'll regret giving it away; I can't let you do that."

"Well, that's mighty thoughtful of you, buddy. But why don't you just take a look inside before you decide to pass."

I picked it up and flipped through the pages. It didn't take long. There were only a handful of them.

"Not exactly *Grey's Anatomy*, is it?" he chortled. "So you can believe that I have it committed to memory, right? It looks really simple, but I guarantee, dude, if you use these pages, it'll keep you on course. *Use these pages every day, and I swear to you, you'll never stray.* Pops and I came up with that. It was our own little jingle."

"All right," I laughed, "I will. But not because of the jingle, I want you to know."

"One more thing, Steve. Pops and I always meant this to be a living document. We knew it wasn't really done, that there'd always be more to put in. So, I'd like you to do me a favor, if you wouldn't mind."

"Anything, Edg. Name it," I said without hesitation.

"As time goes on, as you continue to grow, to learn, to get into and out of trouble..."

"Sounds like me."

He smiled. "... I'd like you to add your thoughts to this book. Farber-ize it. Make it yours, too."

I was honored, of course, but mostly just flat-out stunned. I squirmed.

"I'm not sure that's gonna happen, Edg. But if I really think I have something to contribute, I will. And only because you asked me to."

"Thank you. You're a good man, Mr. Steve. I'm happy to have known you."

"Wait, wait, wait a minute!" I exclaimed. "I'm not quite ready to say good-bye here. I've just got one question for you, all right? It's a little thing, but it's making me nuts. Will you grant me just one last question, oh great, wise, and mysterious Edg? Okay?"

"Okay. Sure. As reward for your acerbic sarcasm. Go ahead."

"Okay," I said, mentally rubbing my hands together like a little kid. "What's the story behind your name? It's gotta be a nickname—but for what?"

"Well," he said with a little smirk. "It's kind of a contraction between my first and last name: Ed G."

"But," I started tentatively. "Pops's last name was Maritime, so yours is, too—right?"

"Pops's last name was the same as mine, but it wasn't Maritime. Not really."

"What?"

"Pops had a great sense of humor, that's what."

"Huh?"

"When I was a kid, I loved the comic book *Richie Rich*. All the characters' names were a reflection of who they were. Richie Rich was, obviously, rich. Lotta was big, remember, as in a whole lotta girl?"

"Yeah? So?"

"So, when I was about eight, Pops started his boat leasing business."

"Yeah?"

"*Maritime*, dude! He went by the name of William G. Maritime. It just stuck. G is the first letter of his real name, and, of course, mine too."

"Get outta here!" I cried. "You can't be serious! What a hoot!"

"It's been our private joke for almost all my life. Now you're in on it, too, and I expect you to protect our sacred secret," he said with mock gravity. At least I think it was mock.

"Okay, then," I said, "so what's the G stand for?"

"Really, Steve," he said, "you're kidding, right?"

"What do you mean?"

"You know what it stands for."

Yeah. I guess I did.

Later On

■ TWENTY-SEVEN

The plane was coming in for a landing over Grand Rapids. I looked out the window at the Midwestern landscape, which spread out below us like a beach of light white snow. On to the next gig: a four-day executive off-site session where I would be holed up somewhere in the wilds of the Michigan countryside with 15 senior managers of a manufacturing company. Odd as it might sound, I was genuinely jazzed at the thought.

Several months had passed since I'd said good-bye to Edg at Pops's trailer. I had tried to see him one more time before he left town. I'd driven back to Point Loma, back to that stately Tudor home with the ivy and stained glass window. This time, I'd bounded boldly up to the door and rung the bell. This time, I'd pounded on that door when no one answered. And this time, the door to the home of Teddy Garrison had finally swung open.

Sadie leapt through the doorway, jumped up, and licked her wet tongue across my face. "Down, girl! Mind yer manners!" he called from inside. "You'd make for a lousy watchdog, I'll tell ya that."

And with that, Smitty the Sign Reader stepped up to the threshold.

"Well, hi, hello, how are ya?" he said when he saw me standing there. "C'mon in and take a load off, Mr. Farber."

I followed Smitty to the back of the house and into the informal dining area off the kitchen. I could see the gazebo through the beveled windows. Two cups of coffee sat steaming on the cherry wood table.

"Nah, I ain't no psychic. I didn't know you were comin'. I already have company is all. Here, have a seat, and I'll get you a mug." He walked into the kitchen.

The bathroom door opened and Janice walked in, pulled up her chair, and sat next to me.

"Hi there," she said, leaning over to give me a hug. "So, you found him."

"Uh-huh. So did you, apparently. Why didn't you just tell me where he lived?" I asked, feigning annoyance.

"I don't know. It was too obvious. I'd already looked for him here with no luck."

Smitty delivered my coffee and sat down across from us. We all looked at each other.

"Well," he said with a cowboy grin, "here we are!"

"He's gone, isn't he?" I asked.

"Yep," said Smitty. "Mr. Ed 'Teddy' Garrison has done vamoosed to whiter shores and bluer waves. I'm lookin' after the place while he's gone. Which, by the way, could be quite a while."

Ed "Teddy" Garrison. Edg, the son of Pops Maritime. Surfer, businessman, philosopher, friend, and advisor. It had all come together for me when I had held the two notes side by side and seen the striking similarities in the handwriting. The kind of similarity that's often there between father and son.

"So, by the time you had asked me to look for him," I said to Janice, "he had already found me."

"Sure looks that way," she said.

"So he engineered this whole thing," I said sounding more annoyed than I felt. "He approached me knowing that you and I were close, and that I would ultimately use his guidance to help you. I can't believe it."

"He didn't use you, Steve, if that's what's bothering you."

She was right, of course. Edg had said in the beginning that I'd be doing him a favor, that we'd be helping each other. If Janice had known I was hanging out with Garrison, she would have been so caught up trying to get him back that she'd have blown her opportunity for greatness. And if I had known, I'd have felt like a middleman, and I really wouldn't have learned a thing. And the value of what I learned was absolutely immeasurable.

"Aw, well, who the heck knows?" quipped Smitty. "Maybe it was all just a happy coincidence."

"Hey, Smitty?" I said.

"Yeah?"

"Read the signs, man." I said it so it sounded like *sahns*.

I stood up in front of the executive team and handed out the materials for the off-site meeting. These folks were engineers, mostly, and predominantly male. Good, salt-of-the-earth, no-nonsense, hardworking human beings who ran a company of 5,000 people fitting the same general profile. We had worked together before, this team and I, so they could tell right away that something was different. The last binder that we had used contained around 250 pages of text, quotes, and worksheets. Once they returned to work, it made for a great doorstop. This one had 13 pages.

"Okay, folks," I said, "let's get started. Here's the operative question for you and your company: How are we going to change the world?"

Part Two
The Radical Edge

"Love All Serve All"

—The Hard Rock Café

"There are many people who think they want to be matadors, only to find themselves in the ring with 2,000 pounds of bull bearing down on them, and then discover that what they really wanted was to wear tight pants and hear the crowd roar."

—Terry Pearce

■ EVEN LATER ON

I was stuck deep in the wilds of Michigan, in the middle of winter, on the back end of a raging snowstorm that had left the countryside covered in—what do poets like to call it?—"a downy soft blanket of white." That sounds much nicer than "a blinding, frozen wasteland," which is a much more accurate image. I wasn't exactly stranded out on the tundra, however, I was holed up in a toasty conference room inside a quaint but efficient bed and breakfast built for the burgeoning corporate off-site market. Moreover, I wasn't alone because I was facilitating an executive retreat for, and I mean this in the nicest way, a roomful of middle-aged, white guys named "Jim."

Blatant gender and ethnic homogeneity aside, this was a group of very intelligent, dependable and steadfast mid- to senior-level managers of a large Cedar Rapids-based manufacturing company, and I was an experienced and newly re-energized leadership consultant on a mission. The group was thrashing around trying to come to terms with a question that I had just dropped on them like a sack of salt on the roadway. It wasn't the kind of question that they teach in facilitator school—such as, for example, "Who would like to volunteer to jump out of a tree?"— but a question that demanded the group look at their role and their company's role from an entirely different perspective. A question that required a very deep level of thought and reflection as well as a steroidal dose of intellectual and moral courage, and that reflected my new perspective on the nature of meaningful life and work in the 21st century:

"How are we going to change the world?"

Apparently, it was a question that invited the inner cynic frothing with spittle and ablaze with venom to emerge, as well.

"Are you kidding me? What kind of question is that?" raged Jim.

"Ummm, a really important one?" I offered.

"How is that supposed to help me with my ridiculous workload, Steve? I mean, c'mon."

"Look," said another Jim. "I think it's a good question. I think we should be willing to consider it at least. It'll make for a good discussion, anyway." Several Jims nodded in support.

"Hold on," said Cynical Jim. "I don't think this is just about having a discussion." He looked at me. "I'm assuming that you don't want us to just talk about how we're going to change the world, you want us to do it. Am I right?"

"Yeah. That's about right."

"One question for you, then, Steve."

"Okay."

"Assuming that we spend the time on this instead of the other really important questions that we need to address at this meeting, and assuming that we actually come up with an answer—"

"Good assumptions," I encouraged.

"Okay, then here's the question I'll want answered. What, exactly, does a person like me need to do to make it all happen?"

"You mean what do you personally have to do to change the world?"

"As long as we're asking the deep questions, yeah."

"And another thing," said another Jim. "We do have a business to run here. Are we just supposed to forget about that while we're out changing the world?"

"Yeah," said yet another, "not to mention having something resembling a personal life in our spare time."

I paused. I looked out the window. I looked back at Jim. I opened my mouth. I closed it again. These were damned good questions.

I wished I had the answers.

A WUP Upside
the Head

■ TWENTY-EIGHT

The Mission Beach area of San Diego is a bit different from Michigan, especially in the wintertime, and I was desperately trying to get back there after my conference with the Jims. There are no direct flights from Grand Rapids to San Diego International Airport, unless you had enough cake to hire your own personal jet which, of course, I didn't. I was prowling the sleek metal and glass halls of O'Hare and killing time as I waited for my connection, which was delayed for an unspecified amount of time. I had ignored the gate agent's admonishment to "remain comfortably seated in the boarding area" in case the weather gods suddenly changed their game plan. The airline was having enough trouble negotiating their pilot contracts let alone getting cooperation from the supreme powers that be, so I bugged out to wander the concourse and pump a little blood into my travel weary brain cells.

I had a lot to think about. The meeting had gone okay, I guess. They had all left thinking much bigger thoughts than what they'd come in with, and I felt really good about that. A shift in perspective is no small thing, to be sure, but I was feeling the dull ache of regret—or was it discontent?—that I used to get after teaching the canned, scripted workshops that were the staples of my earlier days in the leadership development business. Don't get me wrong, I loved the idea of changing the world as the core business and leadership proposition, but I still found myself doubting my ability to actually get it done. I didn't want people to mention the names of Don Quixote and Steve Farber in the same breath. Tilting unabashedly at windmills is one thing; slaying dragons is a whole 'nother smoke.

I turned a corner and found myself face to face with a large and very odd billboard advertisement. It was a picture of a blue Oxford button-down shirt with a red power necktie, and it would have been the classic image of clean, conservative business, if not for one bizarre detail: the tie was on fire. Accompanying it was a big, bold headline that read, "Burn Your Boss" and a tagline at the bottom that said, "Report the use of unlicensed software." This was, essentially, an invitation—no, a challenge—for a person to spy on and rat out their management, and it was punctuated with an 800 number hotline for people to *call right now* and strike the sparkling, gratifying match of revenge.

Now I have as much respect for intellectual property rights as the next guy. Probably more. I'm not a fan of pirating or plagiarism. I sided with Metallica over the early Napster debates and will gladly pop for a buck a song to download to my iPod as opposed to trolling the web for free sources. Software's in the same category, especially on an enterprise level. However, "Burn Your Boss?" Have things really gotten that bad? Did these people honestly expect to tap into some unexpressed reservoir of rage trembling under the surface of other business travelers like myself? More importantly, was this ad working? There was one way to find out. I called the number.

I was hoping to get a live person on the line so I could simply ask the question. What I got, though, was a recorded message saying something about their organization and their office hours followed by an invitation to leave your information—about that evil boss, I assumed—after the tone. As to the question of whether their ad was working, I got my answer right away. Before I could say anything, their machine spoke to me. It said, "You cannot leave a message because the mailbox is full."

■ TWENTY-NINE

I shoveled the gobs of mail from my box, punched in the security code on the front door, and climbed the two flights of stairs to my apartment overlooking Mission Bay. It was always strange to return home to an empty perch and see how much dust had managed to accumulate on the kitchen counters in just one week. The sea air mixed with fine sand always found its way in with or without the security code.

Like scratching for gems in a litter box, I sifted through the mail—junk, bills, a belated birthday card from my dentist, a check from a recent client project—and threw the whole pile on the round oak kitchen table. There was one item that looked a bit more personal, so I picked it up for closer inspection. I tore open the envelope to find a delicate, handcrafted note card from Janice, whom, as you know, I had recently helped out of a sticky career jam. The hand-written words inside the card offered a friendly thinking of you kind of sentiment followed by a postscript reading,

> *"I've given your name to my friend, Rich Delacroix, CEO of Independence Lending Group. He may be calling you for a coaching engagement. He's a nice man. Please don't hurt him."*

She followed it with one of those endearing little emoticons to indicate that she was smiling about that last part.

I rooted around in my empty kitchen but no amount of persistence was going to uncover anything resembling food. As I headed back out the door for a Jack in the Box run, my cell jangled a funky electronic tune.

"Steve Farber?" inquired the voice on the other end of the line. "This is Rich Delacroix. Janice gave me your number. I know this is short notice, but do you, by chance, have time for a quick visit to my office?"

Here in the 21st century, the archetypal call to action mostly comes via the digital phone. Jack, I thought wistfully, would have to wait in his box a little bit longer.

***

Independence Lending Group, Inc.'s (ILGI) snappy commercials promising the best mortgage rates and fastest service on the planet were plastered all over the television and radio airwaves. Maybe they were true; all I knew was that the company had grown like gangbusters during the nuclear boom in the real estate market and the feverish refi activity fueled by subterranean interest rates. I'm usually not impressed by people who make fortunes in bull markets, even though, come to think of it, I never have, but this was one of the few mortgage companies that also managed to survive the subsequent economic meltdown. And *that* was noteworthy.

ILGI's corporate offices were in La Jolla's University Town Center (UTC) neighborhood. UTC is a cement and glass amalgam of apartments, office buildings, malls, restaurants, and a Mormon temple that keeps an impressive and watchful eye over the endless traffic on Interstate 5. I parked my Mustang in the visitor's parking structure and took the elevator up to the 18th floor. The receptionist announced my name into the phone, and before I had a chance to settle into a plush leather chair, Rich Delacroix came bounding through the door on the far end of the waiting area. He was young—mid-30s, I guessed—tan, fit, blond, energetic and, although his attire was casual, exceedingly well-dressed. Despite all that, I liked him immediately.

He gripped my hand with an unsurprising firmness and ushered me into his corner office with a view of the Mormon temple that overlooks the endless traffic on Interstate 5. I got lost for a moment in the symbolic possibilities.

"Steve," he said. "Thanks so much for taking the time to come over. I know you're a busy man with a lot on your plate. So let's get down to it, okay?"

He walked me over to a small conference area in the corner of his corner office, and this time I did sink down into a beautiful, rich, brown leather chair.

"Happy to help if I can, Rich," I said. "What is it that you need?"

"Me, personally? Nothing." I raised my eyebrows, and he hesitated for a moment. "I don't mean it to sound that way, I'm not perfect... that's not what I mean. But I have a very weak link in my management team, and he's the one that really needs help—or that I need help with."

It was really rather endearing to see this supremely self-possessed individual squirm as if he had a tapeworm. This was not a dude who was used to asking anyone for help, let alone a virtual stranger.

"Okay, lay it on me," I said taking out my yellow legal pad. "Give me the whole story."

■ THIRTY

Closer, dealmaker, phone demon, top producer, Cameron Summerfield is a sales god. He came to work at ILGI fresh out of state college where he'd graduated unceremoniously with a liberal arts degree. Armed with a diploma on the wall and the money bug up his butt, he finagled an interview at the exploding mortgage company and, of course, nailed it. He raced through training and attacked the phone with the enthusiasm and compassion of a taunted pit bull, setting a record for new loans in a single month in the first month of his career. His third month on the phone yielded a commission check of $80,000. That's not a misprint, and it was no fluke. Cam was golden week in and week out. He bought a loft in downtown San Diego, a Blaupunkt sound system, and a Porsche Carrera. He was 26 years old.

Now he was the youngest senior vice president in the history of the company. His promotion, it was beginning to seem, being Rich Delacroix's big mistake. The problem, apparently, was really pretty simple: the salespeople, who all ultimately reported to Cam, hated his guts with a steaming passion. Turnover, which was already high in the mortgage industry, was through the roof, and ILGI's best sales talent was bailing at an alarming rate.

"Why? What's he doing that's so despicable?"

"Look," Rich said. "Don't misunderstand, I happen to like Cam very much, and there's no doubt that he's an extraordinary salesman, but leadership doesn't come as naturally to him as closing deals. I want him to make this work, but he's flat-out brutal with the sales team. I'm a believer in incentives and disincentives, too; I like a little friendly competition among the team. But he takes it all too far."

"I'm going to need you to be more specific, Rich. I could interpret that in all kinds of ways. I mean, brutal is a pretty strong word. He's not, like, jamming wood splints into the soles of people's feet, right? So what does Cam's brutality look like?"

"I'm not going to tell you that right now."

"Really? Why?"

Rich pointed over my shoulder and I looked back as the door swung slowly open. "Okay to come in?" called a voice from the hallway.

"Give us a few more minutes, Cam. Be right with you." The door shut with a quiet click.

"Oh. So you just want me to dive right in, huh?" I paused for a second before continuing. "Tell you what, Rich. I don't really know if I can help or not, but I'll make you a deal. Starting tomorrow morning let me hang out with Cam for a day or so, get to know him a bit. If we hit it off you can start paying me. If we don't get along, we'll part ways and I won't send you a bill."

"Sorry," he replied. "I'm a little confused. You want to hang out with him? What does that have to do with coaching?"

"Do me a favor," I said. "Go over to your computer and Google executive coach." He remained seated, staring at me. "C'mon. Humor me."

Rich walked over to his desk, typed the words on his keyboard, and hit return.

"How many hits?" I asked.

He raised his eyebrows. "3,520,000."

"Add another 700,000 or so for leadership coach and 130 grand for management coach and you get the picture, right? Listen, Rich, there are a lot of great coaches out there and some very fine coaching associations and curricula available to those who want to learn how to coach. But anyone can hang out a shingle on the Web and spend an hour a week on the phone with a client, and any one of them would be more than happy to work with Cam."

"Okay..."

"I won't, though, unless..."

"Unless what?" Rich interrupted.

I shrugged. "Unless I like him."

■ THIRTY-ONE

I was flying once from New York to San Francisco after conducting a workshop in which I'd talked nonstop for two straight days. Now I'm not saying it was two days of sparkling verbal gems, mind you, but talk takes energy and mine was gone. Cashing in my first-class upgrades and relaxing in total, blissful silence with a good novel was what I desired the most. Golden ticket in hand, I stood in the boarding line and watched as they loaded up the families traveling with small children contingent. Inching toward the Jetway, a young woman dragged her squirming little boy by the hand. He wailed and howled at the top of his lungs as though she were tearing off his little digits one by one.

Having traveled with my own kids when they were little, I know how stressful a fussy child can be for the parent. Just as I was thinking how difficult this flight was going to be for the young mom, this guy standing in front of me yelled, "*I knew it! I knew it!* I heard that kid screaming in the terminal and I said, 'that kid's gonna be on my flight!' *I knew it.* It never fails!"

What a jerk, I remember thinking. That poor woman was feeling bad enough already. She needed this jerk's vociferous commentary as much as she needed a rabid hyena strapped to her leg.

A few minutes later I walked on the plane and to my horror I realized who my seatmate was: The jerk. I felt like screaming *I knew it! Every time there's a jerk on the plane they end up next to me!* But I didn't. Instead, I sat down, buckled up, pulled out my book, and locked my eyes on the pages. I sent out megatons of don't talk to me vibes and felt confident there was no way he would dare to reach through my pulsating, death star force field. He couldn't possibly have the gall to...

"Hey! Waddaya reading? Oh! I read that book! I've read everything by that guy! Do you live in Frisco or are you going there to work? Man, am I glad I'm not sitting next to that *kid*. Did you hear that kid screamin'? Hey! Waddaya wanna drink?" He waved a hand in the air. "Waitress! They hate that, har-har-har! We are ready to start *drinkin'*!"

This situation is what's known in behavioral psychology circles as a lost cause, so I closed my book, accepted the drink, resigned myself to several hours of pressurized cabin torture, and threw myself at the mercy of the verbose and soon to be plastered Jerk Man. Funny thing is, I had a great time.

Sure, Jerk Man was a bit over the top. He was too loud, and, yeah, he had the emotional intelligence of a bottle nose fly, and I don't mean that in a judgmental way, but he was interesting, eccentric, and a gifted raconteur. In short, by the time we landed in San Francisco, I was glad I'd met him.

"Pretty funny," said Rich. "I assume you're telling me this for a reason?"

"Yeah. Of course. Let me ask you a question with a ridiculously obvious answer. Why was Jerk Man talking to me?"

"What do you mean?"

"I mean why was he talking to me and not the guy sitting back in 10C?"

Rich furrowed his eyebrows. "Ummm... because he was sitting next to you?"

"Right. I was strapped in next to him and not going anywhere for several hours. We talked and got to know each other for one simple, profoundly obvious reason: I was there."

"Okay," mumbled Rich, still not seeing my point.

"Proximity. Physical nearness. Face to face and shoulder to shoulder, Rich. That's the only way to really connect with another human being because that's the only way we really get to know each other."

"And that's why you want to hang out with Cam."

"And that's why I want to hang out with Cam."

"Okay, I get it, Steve. One question, though: after hanging out with Cam, talking with him, getting to know him, what if you don't like him? Does that really mean that you won't work with him?"

"I wouldn't worry about that."

"Why?"

I grinned. "Because I like everybody."

■ THIRTY-TWO

Rich punched a button on his phone and a few minutes later Cam threw the door open and sauntered into the office. He looked like—how can I say this nicely—a cocky GQ wannabe. He wore tasseled loafers, wool pants with razor-sharp pleats, a silk shirt, and enough hair products to slick a porcupine. He may as well have been wearing a sign saying, *I make money.* I really do try to resist snap judgments, but my first thought, I have to admit, was *Danger, Will Robinson!* I stood up and shook his hand as Rich made the introductions.

"So," said Cam as he gave me the once-over, "I understand you're going to give me some of the latest, cutting-edge sales techniques. I'm all ears for anything that'll keep me on top of my game, dude."

I looked at Rich. "Sales techniques?"

He flushed. "Well, Cam, that's not exactly what I had in mind by inviting Steve to work with you."

Cam stiffened as if someone had just stuck a live wire down his Armanis. "What do you mean?" The question caught in his throat. "What's goin' on here?"

"I'm more of a leadership coach, Cam. Extreme Leadership," I said in a Bond, James Bond sort of way. "Rich has asked me to help you get a handle on leading your sales team."

"Why?" he asked, shooting a look at Rich.

"Look, Cam," Rich began. "It couldn't hurt for you to expand your skills in that area. We all know that you're *the man* when it comes to selling. No one's going to argue that point. But... you've got to get your leadership act together if you're going to be a part of this company's future. Don't act as if this is a total surprise. It's not like we haven't talked about this before, right?"

Now it was Cam's turn to flush. I watched the redness rise from his neck to his ears to the top of his forehead. *Thar she blows!* I thought. Then as quickly as his skin had erupted, the color dissipated and he regained his composure.

"Okay, sure, fine. Whatever," he huffed. "When do we start?"

"Tomorrow morning," I said.

"And what do we do first?"

"We have breakfast."

■ THIRTY-THREE

The morning was gray and overcast; the kind of day that gives June Gloom its name. This was December, however, and the Mission Beach coastline was doing that water and sand thing without the slightest inclination or care about what my day was going to be like. I don't know why I love gray beach days, maybe it's because they make me look differently at the pounding waves and squawking seagulls. The birds and the waves don't care if the sun's out or not. That's not a bad attitude for a human to adopt.

Just before the north end of Mission Beach turns into Pacific Beach, Mission Café abuts the boardwalk. You can get a cup of coffee and a muffin and sit right outside where the action is. Cam and I found a spot at a table behind the short retaining wall that separated the porch from the boardwalk. I took in a full, deep breath of sea air. Man, what could be better? My morning coffee, steaming and potent; the Pacific, rolling and churning; the beach walkers, strolling and talking, all of it reminding me—not that I needed it— of how much I loved this place. The air smelled of suntan lotion, which told me that despite the cloud cover, the early morning crowd was characteristically optimistic.

I'm always amazed by the variety of earnest morning walkers: college kids clipping along in their baseball caps, cargo shorts, and tight-laced Adidas, older folks glad still to be walking at all, skaters on their boards, and bikers riding backwards on their handlebars. It's quite a parade— not the kind that would have inspired John Philip Sousa, but I never really cared for his music anyway.

All this I kept to myself. Cam, however, was more external with his thoughts than I was. I slowly realized that he was spewing forth an endless stream of color commentary on the overweight, over-thin, over-plasticized, over—or under—whatever of every person passing by. He didn't realize it, but he was pushing my buttons as rapidly and aggressively as a rat beeping a scientist for food. It didn't sound like anger so much as condescension, arrogance, and an overall *these people suck* perspective on the scene.

"Jeez! Look at *that* guy. Can you believe him? He looks like a dog I used to own. Get a load of that hair. What a fleabag!" He gave me a conspiratorial nudge on the arm. "What sewer did he sleep in last night?"

The current object of Cam's attention was, indeed, a little scruffy looking, I suppose. He was tall and wiry, and his too-tan arms poked out from the cutoff sleeves of a blue tie-dyed T-shirt. Green khaki cargo shorts and Reef flip-flops completed what was a fairly run-of-the-mill beach ensemble. However, it was his amazing hair that set him apart from the rest of the crowd: prolific red dreadlocks fell down from the top of his head, and, beginning just beneath a wide, prominent nose, which held up round, lemon yellow sunglasses, a giant, red mustache and beard stuck out in all directions at once. As if on cue, the sewer dog in question launched himself over the retaining wall, scooped up a chair, and swung it over to our table. He sat down next to Cam and across from me as though we'd been expecting him all along. Truth was I had. If our visitor's unruly, red beard really had been casting off fleas, Cam's mouth would have caught them all.

"Here's the funny thing, Cam," I said, enjoying his shock. "This fleabag here is a friend of mine, and, it just so happens, he's our breakfast date." I could feel my smile broadening as I watched Cam digest this bit of news.

Smitty grinned at Cam and then bear slapped me on the back like he always did. "Farberoni, my man, it's a great day to be alive and kickin', especially considering the alternative." Smitty's laugh is infectious. It starts somewhere deep down in his body and seems to ripple all the way to the ends of each red hair—and that's a lot of rippling. Cam, however, looked as if he was afraid of other infectious things.

"Smitty, I'd like you to meet Cam; Cam, my friend Smitty here is one of the wisest people I've ever met, and I'm not embarrassed to say so."

"And I ain't embarrassed to hear you say it. It's a pleasure, Mr. Cam," Smitty said, extending his tan, weathered hand. Cam shook it without much exuberance, but Smitty wouldn't let go. He gripped Cam's hand as if he was trying to squeeze a marble out of a fish. "Dang, son! You look a lot peppier than you are." Smitty leaned in close to Cam and whispered, "You been drinkin' your milk?"

Cam's face reddened and he squeezed back.

"Don't get angry now, son," said Smitty. "I'm just messin' with ya. Now why don't you order me a coffee, here, Farberama. And get this boy a glass of moo juice. I'll be right back. The lizard's barkin', if you know what I mean." He jumped up and ran off to find the public terrarium, if I knew what he meant.

"What the hell was *that* all about?" hissed Cam. "Are you really expecting me to waste my time like this? I thought you were supposed to be coaching me." He said *coaching* like he was he was trying to eject something nasty from the back of his throat.

I gazed out at the water and calmly replied. "Listen, Cam. Give Smitty a chance; you may be surprised what you can learn from him. Appearances aren't always what they seem, right?"

"Wait a minute," he said in amazement. "I just thought that he was your friend. Are you trying to tell me that he's here to help me? This is a joke, right?" He waited for me to answer. "Right?"

Smitty returned much faster than I'd thought possible, but there he was parking himself next to Cam and cozying in nice and close.

Cam leaned back in his chair. "What is this?" he said looking over at Smitty. "*A Christmas Carol?* When do I meet the ghosts of breakfasts past and future?"

Well, well! Cam has a sense of humor. I had to admit I was impressed by his joke, despite the spiteful tone.

"Something bothering you, son?" said Smitty. "Is there something you wanna say to me?"

"Yeah."

"Well go on, then."

"Stop calling me son."

"Sorry, Buck. I don't mean nothin' by it. Just a Texas habit. So tell me a little about yourself."

"Like what?" Cam said with a sniff.

"Well, for starters: where'd you go to school?"

"San Diego State. Graduated with a degree in Sorority Relations and I was immediately brought into ILGI where I decided pretty damn quickly to take no prisoners. Four years later, I'm 26, I'm senior vice president of a mortgage company with over 1,000 people on the payroll and it's up to me to make sure we're closing deals and writing loans. And I've got my boys and girls whipped into shape." He popped his sleeve over the enormous watch on his wrist.

"Alright, then. You like to read? Read any management stuff?" Smitty asked, as he started mixing half a dozen packets of sugar into his coffee.

Cam raised his eyebrows at the empty sugar packets collecting one by one on the table. "I don't have time to read books that tell me what I already know. Not to sound arrogant or anything but I've got, like, instinct or something. You can't teach that. I can smell a deal. All I need is that feeling, and... BAM... another client for the company and money in my pocket. And, by the way, it's not chump change I'm talking about."

"Well, Buck, I'll bet you just about got it all, then— the Porsche, the kick-ass apartment in the city, designer clothes, martinis at The Bitter End, steaks at Donovan's, and more bling for your many young ladies then they could wear in a year. That about right?"

"That's about right, *Buck*." Cam said proudly looking my way. "Can we go now? I've got a sales team to run."

"Now hold on a minute, there, Buck!" hollered Smitty. Several people at other tables looked our way to see what the fuss was about, and Smitty instinctively lowered the volume on his Texas boombox voice.

"Just relax," he said quieter. "You're getting the wrong idea. You're thinkin' that I'm some kinda money's-the-root-of-all-evil kinda guy. That I'm gonna tell you that the pursuit of material things is shameful. And that you're a shallow, shallow little boy."

Cam shrugged indifferently. "I don't really care what you think of me, to tell you the truth. But, yeah, that's what it sounds like, and I don't need a lecture in ethics. There's nothing wrong with the way I live, so butt out."

This was not going quite as well as I'd hoped.

"Smitty," I interrupted. "Fair's fair. Since you're giving Cam the third degree, why don't you tell him a bit about your background?"

"You betcha. Happy to oblige." He turned to Cam. "Ever hear of a little company called Maritime?"

"Maritime and Son? Sure, who hasn't?"

"I was CIO."

■ THIRTY-FOUR

Cam just about swallowed his tongue. "You were the chief information officer of Maritime and Son?" he asked incredulously.

"No, sir, I was not."

"But you just said..."

"I said CIO, not chief information officer. Really, Buck, do I look like the type?" And here came the rippling, deep laughter that I loved so much. "I was the clear insight officer, is what I was. Yeah, yeah, I know it sounds contrived, but William Maritime himself gave me the title, Buck, and that was back before those kinds of titles were trendy. So I wasn't about to argue, and you wouldn't have neither."

The name of William Maritime got Cam's attention, and for good reason. Maritime, known as Pops to his friends, was a business legend and a builder of fortunes. I was fortunate enough to have connected with him personally just before he passed away. In retrospect, my brief meeting with Pops had been the most valuable afternoon of my life.

"My job, Buck, was to keep the company awake, alive, and alert to the world outside the walls of the Maritime empire. 'The only way to change the world is to be fully in it, my young friend,' is what Pops said to me when I first joined on as an intern in my last summer as a graduate student. So, I tried to live fully in the world—to watch, stay awake, pay attention, and try to extract meaning and significance from everything I saw. Then I'd go back to the company and share what I'd learned. I became what you might call the corporate anthropologist, the applied futurist. Once upon a time, I explained to Farber here that I'm a sign reader. I take the lay of the land and all its inhabitants runnin' around it, and then try and see things, with as much clarity as I can muster, from their perspective. That's how you keep learnin' and that's how you get and keep a radical edge in your business and in your life overall."

Cam raised an eyebrow. "And they paid you for that?"

"Mucho dinero, Buck. And worth every shekel, if I do say so m'self. Which I do."

"Let me get this straight," he said with not a little bit of skepticism. "You're telling me that Mr. Maritime paid you a small fortune to what? Observe things?"

Smitty winked at me from behind his yellow shades. "I

never said small."

"Not that it really matters, Cam," I said. "But Smitty's done all right for himself. Now do yourself a favor and just listen to him for a minute, will you, please?" I could feel the stiletto heels of impatience tap-dancing on the back of my neck.

"All right, then!" crowed Smitty as he clapped his hands together. "Let's start with the basics. First of all, you have to do what you can to learn from the great ones. Make sense?"

Cam nodded. "To tell you the truth, back when I first started working at ILGI, I listened to a ton of sales training audios—Hopkins, Waitley, Gitomer, guys like that."

"Excellenté. Courses can help, but did you know that Farber here is one of the great ones?"

Cam looked at me and I looked at Smitty. I could feel my face reddening. "Well, that's nice of you to say, Smitty, but I'm not that special. I'm just trying to..."

"Hush up," he said, "and let me finish."

I sat quietly in the glow of the unexpected and deeply satisfying compliment.

Smitty pointed out toward the beach. "See that tourist with the high-top sneakers? Also one of the great ones. The lady with the mouthful of cheese Danish at the table over there? A great one if ever there was one." He jabbed his finger through the air at every person walking by on the boardwalk. "Great, great, great, great."

And I swear he'd still be sitting there great-ing away if

Cam hadn't reached out and snatched Smitty's finger in his hand.

"Okay, I get what you're saying. *We're all great ones*," Cam oozed in a cynical, syrupy voice.

"Yeah, I knew that," I mumbled.

"This ain't no platitude, boys." I noticed that Smitty had made me a part of his audience. "If you assume that you can learn from anyone—if you assume that you must learn from *everyone*—then everyone becomes a great teacher for you. Even if someone's a slime sucking scumbag of a leech, they qualify for greatness if you can learn something from them."

"Okay then," said Cam. "I'm a kick-ass 26-year-old sales executive. Let's see what you can learn from me."

That got my goat right in the sweets. "Let's get clear on the concept, Cam," I growled through my teeth. "I'd like you to see what you can learn from Smitty, not the other way around."

"Bad Farber!" Smitty admonished in a dog trainer tone. "He's got a good point. No doubt that we all have much to learn from you, Buck, and I'd love to hear your whole story sometime in the very near future."

"It's Cam."

"For right now, though, Cam, I got something that'll help both you and Mr. Farberacious here to become CIOs yourselves."

"Sounds cool to me," I said. I always found Smitty's perspective refreshing and surprising. To him, good advice was everywhere; you just had to be alert enough to notice and care enough to ask yourself the right questions about the nature of the world and its inhabitants. A sudden smacking pain on my right ear jolted me back to attention.

"Yow! Jeez, Smitty, what the hell'd you do that for?" I yelped, palming my ear. He had slapped me on the side of the head with a small spiral-bound notebook, which now lay innocently on the table in front of me.

Smitty laughed, which really ticked me off. "Aw, c'mon now, Stevie. That was just a friendly little WUP upside your head. We all need that from time to time, don't we?"

"Yeah, well, I read 'A Whack on the Side of the Head' a long time ago, Smitty." I said fondling my ear, more from shock than from pain. "But I don't think it was supposed to be taken literally."

"Whack, wup, smack, all the same idea. We gotta keep ourselves from falling asleep at the wheel. Sometimes literally, but, you're right-o, Farbo, I was just makin' a point in my own impish but endearing sort of way." He picked up the little notebook—aka weapon—and dangled it in front of Cam and me. "This ain't a notebook; it's a WUP."

"A WUP," I repeated. Cam let out a deep sigh and looked at his watch.

"Yup, a WUP. Stands for Wake-Up Pad, and it's the most important little life shifter that you're ever gonna find, if you use it right. Matter of fact, if you don't use it right it is just another notebook. But if you do," he leaned close to Cam, "it'll bring you more money than you have *ever* made, my young Rock-a-fella."

"Explain," said Cam with slightly more enthusiasm

than he'd shown so far, which wasn't saying much.

"In a minute," he said and then looked my way. "And you, Farbio, are takin' up the call to change the world for the better, eh?"

"Trying to."

"Good! But you know what?" He waggled his WUP. "You ain't gonna get nowhere without the wisdom contained in this little puppy right here."

"Smitty. C'mon," I said, awakening the skeptic within. "I don't see what difference a notebook is…"

"It's a WUP!" he boomed. "*A Wake-Up Pad*. Here, take it." He shoved it at me. "Open'er up and look at what's inside."

Okay, I mused, *there's got to be something really extraordinary in this thing*. Starting to feel a little jolt of anticipation, I slowly turned the card stock cover to reveal the first page of Smitty's WUP. It was extraordinary.

Extraordinarily blank.

■ THIRTY-FIVE

While I was staring, incredulous, at that blank sheet of paper, Rich Delacroix had just started a senior management meeting in the oak paneled conference room at the national headquarters of Independence Lending Group, Inc. The topic at hand, I would later find out, was the uncertain future of one Cam Summerfield, SVP of sales.

"Folks," said Rich, "I want your help with the impend-ing crisis on the sales team. If things don't change soon, we're going to lose a lot of good people and it's going to be a real bitch to hit the numbers we need for the next expansion phase."

"Isn't that what we pay Cam for?" asked Sharon Washington, SVP of underwriting. "Shouldn't he be here for this discussion?"

"Yes, he should," said Rich, "except for one small thing." He raised his eyebrows and exhaled a sigh ripe with the unspoken but obvious reality.

"Cam is the problem." Sharon completed the thought for him.

"Do we have anyone else ready to step in for Cam?" A fidgety, uncomfortable silence permeated the room as the implications of Rich's question hit home.

"Are you going to fire him?"

"Not necessarily. He's got one last chance to start getting his leadership act together."

"How long are we giving him to show some improvement?"

"One day."

"Generous," Sharon oozed. "What if," she continued sarcastically, "he doesn't get hit by lightning, or his lobotomy doesn't take? Are you going to fire him?"

"No," Rich replied. "Worse. I'm going to demote him."

■ THIRTY-SIX

"Let me see that." Cam snatched the notebook—sorry, WUP—away from me, looked at it, and slapped it back down on the table. "Listen," he demanded, "very, very carefully: I... don't... have... time... for... this. I'm going back to work," he said to me, "and I'm telling Rich that this didn't work out. Smitty, it's been a real treat, but I'm outie." He pushed his chair back and stood up.

Smitty rose with him, put his hands on Cam's shoulders, and gently pushed him back into his seat.

"Relax, dude," he said in a surprisingly calm voice. "Just hear me out for a minute. I'm gonna tell you how to use this thing, and then you decide if you're innie or outie." It wasn't a request, and he didn't give Cam a chance to protest.

"Number one," Smitty began as he picked up the WUP, "carry this with you at all times. Now a Wake-Up Pad doesn't have to be paper. You could use your iPad, laptop, or a voice recorder on your cell, but just to get the practice down, start with this little book until it becomes like another appendage like your hand or your—well, let's just say your hand.

"Go on," he pushed a pen into Cam's hand. "Write that down: carry at all times." His eyes bored into Cam until he complied.

"Number two." He waited until Cam wrote the number on the pad. "Scan, just like you were a computer scanner. Your scanner just copies; it doesn't comment, it doesn't offer an opinion, it doesn't tell you you're stupid for wasting your time on that photo of the girl you met while y'all were dancin' on the bar at Jimmy Love's. Just scan your environment and record what you see. Scan the bestseller lists and notice what people are reading; scan the magazine racks and pick up publications that don't interest you like, I dunno, *The Tattoo Review* or *Graffiti Today*; scan the weekly TV show rankings; scan the headlines of your online newsfeeds and actual print-and-ink newspapers from 20 different cities; scan what's trending on Twitter; scan the room that you're sitting in; scan the crowd as you're toolin' down the street during your lunch break. Then, every so often, write down what you're seeing in your WUP. Write down your observations of subcultures that are entirely alien to you and trends in the tastes of the popular culture. Capture little ideas, snapshots of natural, political, and social phenomena. Scan, scan, scan. Look at everything going on around you and write your observations in the pad."

"And then what?" Cam asked. "What's the point?"

Smitty held up a finger. "I'm coming to that, but at first all you're doing is scanning the world and writing down what you see without comment or judgment."

I thought about Cam's earlier scathing commentary on the beach population. "What do you mean by no judgment?" I asked, trying to lead Smitty in a direction that I thought Cam needed to be taken.

"I mean," he said looking right at Cam. "That I ain't no flea infested guttersnipe, am I, Buck?"

"I'll give you that." Cam conceded. "My first impression of you was wrong."

"Well, now, ain't you the big man for admittin' it? And that's the point, my repentant friend. Observe but don't judge. You might have written a description of me in your WUP, but you'd have left out the arrogant, holier-than-thou attitude. You with me?"

"Yeah," muttered Cam, letting the insult pass like gas in the breeze.

"All right, then. Let's move on to number three."

■ THIRTY-SEVEN

"Tell me the truth now, Cammie Boy. Have you ever listened in on another person's conversation? Let's say you're standing in line at Starbucks, minding your own business, and there's a couple behind you in line having a little tiff about something or other; his mother, her aerobics instructor, something like that. Tell me that you're not going to listen in."

Cam shrugged. "Yeah, I am."

"Good! Of course you would. Everyone would! You know why? We're interested in the drama of humanity, especially dramas we're not supposed to know anything about. We love those little windows into others' lives. So, I say this: eavesdrop away! We do it anyway, so why not make it a habit and a practice, and listen in with conscious intent?"

"Say what?" I chirped.

"Oh relax, Farberoosky. I'm not talking about buggin' peoples' offices or anything like that. This is nothin' more than paying attention to what other people are talkin' about. Hell, listening to talk radio is a form of eavesdropping, ain't it? Tune in to both right and left-wing shows and you'll pretty much be listening in on an entire national conversation. *Scan* and *eavesdrop* are basically just lookin' and listenin'. Consider yourself both a scanner and a microphone. Again, you're not making any judgments on what you're seeing or hearing, just collectin' the data that's coming to you.

"Okay, now, the next thing you do is..." Smitty paused and looked at Cam until he got the nonverbal message, picked up his pen, and wrote a nice, clean number four in his evolving WUP. "... *Ponder*. After collecting your observations for a while you stop, read it over, and give it some reflection. What are the implications of this? What can I learn from that? Why are so many people doing X, and what might that mean for all of us?

"For example, why are so many people watching reality TV? And why doesn't anyone seem to notice that the phrase reality TV is the ultimate oxymoron? Or maybe one day you were royally ticked off because you were tryin' to do some work on your vacation, but you couldn't get your laptop to connect. So, you had jotted down a note in your WUP that said something like I can't find a flippin' WiFi connection when I really need one. So now you ask the question, what are the implications of anytime, anywhere broadband Internet connections and what's that gonna mean for the way we should sell mortgages in the near future? Now, you don't just ask the questions, you think about the answers. We don't give ourselves nearly enough time to reflect. We think we don't have time. But I'm telling you, if all you're doin' is reacting to things rather than giving yourself the time to ponder, you're gonna be left in the dust without any new ideas. And you certainly won't be leadin' the pack, right, Buck?

"So you see what's starting to happen here, boys?" Smitty was making sure that Cam wasn't the only one hearing the message. "You're observing, processing, interpreting, massaging, and playing with your experience of the human drama—or comedy, more likely—and encouraging your brain to look for new, clear insights which will lead, eventually, to new ways of doing things in your business and in your life."

Cam was actually nodding his head. "It's a brain-storming tool," he said.

"Yeah, think of it that way at first, if you want. Whatever it takes to get you to do it is just fine with me," Smitty chortled and winked at me.

I winked back, but I didn't know why.

■ THIRTY-EIGHT

"Now, this next step is where the magic happens," Smitty rolled on. "This is what makes the mondo difference, and it's the one thing that note takers since the days of tablets and chisels have rarely even thought about. So write down and underline number five: *Talk about it.*"

"With who?" asked Cam.

"Yeah," I added, finding myself in Cam's corner. "With whom?" I've always been a stickler about the usage of *who* and *whom*, much to the chagrin of all my friends and family, whom I am incessantly correcting.

"With everyone," said Smitty. "Or everyone that matters, anyway. Talk about your observations and ideas with your team, for example. 'Here's what I'm noticing. What are you seeing?' That kind of thing. Just kick it around and see where the discussion takes you. See what happens over time."

Cam stared at him, slack-jawed. "Talk with my team about... nothing? What are we, *Seinfeld* now?" he choked. "When? During all that spare time we have on our hands? Right! Hey everybody, hang up those phones! Let someone else close those loans for a while so we can go out for lattes and talk about nothing! Are you crazy? Don't answer that."

"You're not talking about nothing; you're talking about everything. Everything you've been observing and thinking about. And you're not doing this to waste time; you're doing this to create new ideas, new ways of serving your customers, and new ways of getting more business. Ultimately, that's what this is all about, Cam, and that's what you really want, isn't it?"

"Yeah, but I don't see how."

"Because you're too dang *linear*, that's why." Smitty interrupted. "You have to give this some time and eventually, and I'll write you a personal guarantee on this, a new idea's gonna pop up and WUP you upside the head. There's no way to know where it's gonna come from. There's no way to predict which conversation will lead to what new idea. But it will happen. You hearin' me?"

"Hearin', just not believin'," Cam replied with a mocking Texas drawl.

"I'm tellin' ya, dude. It'll happen. I mean, back in 1966, Herb Kelleher sketched out the idea for Southwest Airlines on the back of a napkin, for gosh sakes. One day he and his pal Rollin King just started talking and WUP! There it was."

"That's not the same thing," sniffed Cam.

Smitty leaned forward in his chair and slid his wallet out of the back pocket of his cargo shorts. He plucked a wad of bills from inside, rifled through it for a moment, and slapped a crisp, one hundred dollar note on the table in front of Cam. "Go on," he said. "Take it."

Cam reluctantly dragged the bill toward himself, rolling his eyes. "What's the catch?"

"Start using the WUP just like I been describing it to ya'. Do it for a month. Have weekly discussions with your team. Do it even though you think it's an inane idea from a loony old coot."

"And?" Cam was eyeing the C-note.

"And I'll give you ten more of them Franklins just for playin' the game."

I did what they call in the movies a spit-take and spewed coffee on the table. "You're going to pay him a thousand bucks to take your advice?" I cried.

"1,100, actually," said Cam.

"But you gotta promise me one thing," Smitty continued, ignoring me. "When inspiration strikes, when a new, bona fide really great idea presents itself—"

"Yeah?"

"You have to do it; that's number six. That's when the talking comes to a screeching halt and audacious action takes over. Kelleher and King went from idea to Southwest's first route map on the back of that napkin. In other words, my man, I am expecting you to stick your neck out and try something new in your business. Got it?"

"And," Cam folded the bill and stuck it in his shirt pocket, "what if I don't?"

"Then you keep the hundred," Smitty offered. "And the knowledge that you, the big shot dealmaker, super sales guy, wasn't up to this one itty-bitty task. And Farber and I will know the truth about Cameron Summerfield, that he dresses up like a big, strong mover and shaker, but he's really a mewling little boy in short pants and knee socks."

I laughed, I couldn't help it, but so did Cam, which I thought was a pretty good sign. He said, *deal*, and patted the pocket on his finely woven cotton and silk blend shirt.

Smitty turned his attention on me. "Are you getting the full picture here, Farberama? Do you see where the WUP can lead?"

"Yeah, I do. I'm going to give it a try myself."

"Of course you are," he grunted. "And I ain't paying you, so don't even ask. But here's the full picture. Can you imagine, Farber, what it would be like for an entire company to have everybody—and by everybody, I mean *everybody* from the CEO to the receptionist—keep his or her own Wake-Up Pad? And every so often—weekly, monthly, it really doesn't matter—there's a meeting where all that happens is people compare notes and talk about what they're seeing. Then when the ideas start flyin', you capture 'em, and you start trying stuff. That would be a whole company of CIOs. A company that is entirely awake to what's happening outside its walls. Can you imagine that, Farberoni?"

I could imagine it and it brought to mind what Gary Hamel said in his book, *Leading the Revolution*: "Every day, companies get blindsided by the future—yet the future never arrives as a surprise to everyone in the organization. Someone somewhere was paying attention." An entire company of people paying attention. When I really stopped and thought about it, I was damn near awestruck by the potential.

So, I wrote the idea in my WUP, which at the moment was a crumpled napkin.

I jotted down the words *Carry, Scan, Eavesdrop, Ponder, Talk, and Try Something New*, and then wrote, *everyone a CIO? How? What could happen?* I turned to Cam, a vision of millions of CIOs swimming in my head, and asked what he thought of all this.

MY

GET

REWARD

5

"Not now... I'm scanning," he said as he watched a group of startlingly attractive young women walking in a bevy on the beach.

Smitty put his hand on my shoulder and laughed, "Buddy, you got yourself a live one here."

Then, as if goosed by an invisible elf, Smitty jumped up and reached into another of his many cargo pockets. "Hey, I nearly forgot," he said as he rooted about. "Got something for you that I think you're gonna like." He pulled out a folded envelope and handed it to me.

I took it from him and looked it over, front and back. There was no address, return or otherwise.

"I meant to give it to you when we sat down," he said. "But we got all distracted and whatnot. Anyway, you need to read it right now. He said it was real important."

"Who did?"

Smitty grinned. "It's from Edg."

■ THIRTY-NINE

My heart skipped when I recognized the script. I hadn't heard from Edg in the two years since he'd swept into my world and in one eventful week twisted my head and heart around until I got my life back on track. He had opened my eyes to the nature of Extreme Leadership and what it meant to take the Radical Leap—cultivate *love*, generate *energy*, inspire *audacity*, and provide *proof*; insight that had helped me beyond measure. Then, just as suddenly as he'd swooped into my life, he was gone. "Big waves await me at other shores," he had said with his typical, annoying cryptic aplomb. Now he was back, in the form of scratchy blue ink on yellow legal paper. I excused myself from the table and walked down to the shore to spend a few moments catching up with my old friend.

Dear Steve,

The beach I'm sitting on is whiter than talcum and, this time of year, cooler than cool as the sand runs over my feet and through my toes. The waves are perfect here, dude, and the mist coming off the ocean is almost enough to spray away my grief over Pops. But I don't want it to, you know? He was my mentor, my friend, my—is this a word?— shaper. It'll take a hell of a lot more than sea spit to get my mind off him.

It's weird, but I can see him so vividly now that he's gone. Pops left me memories. And feelings. And—okay, I'll say it—a boatload of money. Not that I need it. But the lessons, dude... well... you can imagine.

Pops taught everyone he touched how impor- tant it is to take the radical leap, and there's no doubt that that knowledge will be at the core of his legacy. Pops was the champion of audacity, of the need to have a bold and blatant disregard for normal constraints. But most important was his deep, unwavering devotion to the plight of the human condition and the challenge, joy, and, ultimately, responsibility of the human experience. To be an Extreme Leader, Pops would say, is really nothing more than the challenge to be fully human at work, at home, in the community, and in the world as a whole. And, according to him, to be fully human means that you accept a radical level of personal accountability for making the future markedly better than the present.

Accountability has become an uncomfortable idea; it's that thing that people desperately want other people to take. These people need to be more accountable is an edict that I've heard more times than I care to remember. Pops' message is this: you are accountable. You. Whoever you are. Do you need to enlist other people? Of course. Do you have to make things happen all by your little lonesome? Of course not. Pops didn't build an empire by himself. But he held himself accountable for everything he ever set out to accomplish. And everything he ever set out to accomplish would, if successful, change some piece of the world he touched for the better. That level of accountability, dude, is not simply about being more effective and productive at work. It's not just about achieving goals and accomplishing tasks, and it's not about proving to anyone how wonderful a person you are. It's about living, breathing, toiling, and playing way the hell out there on that radical edge where you simultaneously stoke your business to phenomenal success, amp your life to the loudest possible volume of joy and meaning, and change the world for all of us. Hit all three things at the same time and you've got the Radical Edge as a businessperson and as a human being.

I've been thinking about you, Farber. You and I have a unique connection, and Pops certainly saw something in you, too. So I've been wondering: are you just thinking about Extreme Leadership, or are you ready to skate out on the Radical Edge? I hope you are because if all you want to do is enhance your performance, then burn this letter and go take a class at The Learning Annex.

Agnes used to say, "If you live in this world without ever attempting to change it, you will have sold a ruby for the price of Spam."

That's Agnes. She's a ruby if ever there was one. She owns a diner near the beach in Encinitas called The Wake-Up Call. I spent a lot of hours there when I was a kid, hanging out there under Agnes' watchful eye whenever Pops was traveling, which was pretty damn often. She was a woman who lived on the Radical Edge, and, believe it or not, Pops learned a great deal from her. And so did I. And guess what, so will you.

You need to go talk to Agnes, Farber. Today. Go directly to The Wake-Up Call. Do not pass go; do not collect $200. I've asked Smitty to point you in the right direction. You're gonna love her and

I'm sure the feeling will be mutual. Oh, and one more thing: Don't forget your WUP.

Later dude.

Love,
Edg

■ FORTY

I folded the note and put it in my pocket as I walked back up the beach to rejoin Smitty and Cam at the café. I was thrilled to hear from Edg, and I was excited about meeting this woman, Agnes. She had to be an exceedingly special person to have had such an influence on Edg and Pops. I admit that I would have preferred visiting Agnes alone, but since I'd committed myself to Cam for the day, I reluctantly decided to bring him along. As I got to the table, I noticed that my two dudes seemed to be tolerating each other well enough. Nothing appeared broken, anyway.

"Well, Cam, it looks like we have a lunch date up in Encinitas."

Smitty clapped his hands, pushed his chair back, and jumped to his feet. "You boys are in for a treat. Agnes Golden is one of a kind, and that's a shame for the rest of us. We could use a lot more just like her, that's for sure."

"Who is she?" asked Cam.

"You'll see, Buck. Even you won't be able to resist her charms."

Cam looked at me.

I shook my head. "I don't know her either, Cam, but let's just say she comes highly recommended. And besides, we're going to have to eat lunch anyway, so why not at The Wake-Up Call?"

"From the Wake-Up Pad to The Wake-Up Call, huh? Is that a coincidence, or does everyone in your circle of friends have a fear of sleep?"

"No co-inky-dink, Buck. Agnes named 'em both."

"Well, then," said Cam the all-knowing sales god. "I'm sure this *will* be a treat."

Agnes

■ FORTY-ONE

The Wake-up Call was on the main drag of Encinitas, just two blocks from the ocean. It felt like a small beach community diner but with an impressively brisk lunch business. As I searched for a parking space and scanned the bumpers of the parked cars for the telltale backup light, I noticed that the tables on the sidewalk were packed. The inside clearly was, too, because another crowd was hovering in front of the adjacent boutiques, waiting for their turn.

As luck would have it, and sometimes you're just lucky, I found a spot three blocks south. Cam had suggested that I park closer in a delivery zone and that he'd pay the inevitable ticket to save time. Even though that was an interesting take on valet parking, I decided to play it legal. Besides, a short walk wouldn't hurt either of us.

As we sauntered up the crowded sidewalk toward the diner, I gathered The Wake-Up Call's clientele wasn't the normal touristy bunch. Conversations throughout the patio were in full lunchtime swing and the wait staff moved effortlessly among the tables with plates of food, pots of coffee, and lots of laughter. I got the distinct impression that they all knew each other.

We made our way inside and found the hostess, who was dressed in a flowered T-shirt and khaki shorts and wrapped in a white apron with a name badge that said Mary Ellen in a friendly, festive script. Her blonde hair was pulled back from her perfectly tanned face. She appeared to be in her early 40s, although with her lithe, runner's frame and youthful, energetic demeanor, it wouldn't surprise me if she got carded every now and then.

"Hey, boys, welcome to The Wake-Up Call," she virtually sang. "We've got about a thirty-minute wait right now. Shall I put you on the list for something inside, outside, or the first one that pops up?"

"Actually," I ventured, looking around at the throngs of diners, "Edg sent us to see Agnes. Any chance you can get us in?" Name-dropping never hurts, although I always feel a little guilty trying it.

"Oh, that boy!" Mary Ellen chirped. "I haven't seen him since Pops left us. How is he?"

"He seems to be doing fine." True, as far as I knew. "I'm sure he'd appreciate your asking about him. Is Agnes here?"

"First time at The Wake-Up Call, eh? She's in the back booth, as always. And it looks like she's alone, which is *very* unusual. Can I bring you a..." she sized us up and then pointed a finger at me and said, "a Diet Coke and" a finger at Cam, "a black coffee?"

"Yeah, sure," I said, surprised as Cam nodded in agreement. "How'd you know?"

"Just a little game I like to play. It's no big thing, I'm wrong as often as I'm right, but it doesn't stop me from guessing," she laughed with a disarming burst of joy. "Come with me; I'll tell her you're here."

As she walked us toward the back booth, I saw a tall, slightly plump African-American woman sitting peacefully in a cushioned bench against the wall. As we got closer I realized that "peaceful" was something of an understatement. She was, in fact, sleeping. Her chin slumped slightly toward her chest, and her short, otherwise thick, gray hair was thinning slightly on top, which I knew because that was pretty much all I could see of her as we approached. I marveled at how anyone could take a nap in the middle of all this chaos. Mary Ellen put her hand gently on Sleeping Beauty's shoulder and she straightened immediately, blinking her eyes as though being aroused from a deep thought rather than a slumber. She had to be at least 90 years old, which for some reason caught me entirely off guard. Her dark face was deeply lined, and white, meticulously plucked eyebrows arched playfully over her gray, luminous eyes. "A couple of young studs here to see you, Agnes," Mary Ellen winked at us. "Should I send them away?"

"Oh, you're so bad, girl." Agnes raised her perfect eyebrows at Mary Ellen as she chuckled. She looked Cam and me over as though sizing us up against that stud remark and then gestured for us to sit. I slid into the booth and Cam followed.

Smiling with her whole face, Agnes extended her delicate hand across the table and, feeling myself melting, I took it in mine. "And you are Farber. Don't look so shocked, Smitty called to say you were coming. I know you have a first name, baby, so why do Edg and Smitty call you *Farber?*"

"Not unusual," I said, loving that she called me *baby*. "Most people know me on a last name basis, I guess."

"Well, *Steve's* gonna work just fine for me." She turned toward Cam, who'd been conspicuously silent so far. "And who's this handsome young man?"

Before I could make the introduction, Cam thrust out his hand and said, "I am the prisoner, he is the warden and this," he swept his head around to indicate his surroundings, "is my jail."

Agnes looked at Cam's hand and hesitated ever so slightly before she gripped it in both of hers. "Oh, my," she smiled. "My, my, my."

You got that right, I thought/mumbled to myself.

"Call me Cam, though. Cam Summerfield." He shot Agnes such a charming grin that I almost yelped in surprise. This dude could certainly turn on the charm when he wanted to. It almost seemed—and I mean almost—that he felt guilty about spewing his sarcasm on this innocent old lady.

Mary Ellen arrived with my Diet Coke and Cam's coffee. I picked up my glass and took a sip; Cam did the same with his coffee, except he used his left hand, which almost caused us to have a midair beverage collision.

"You're a lefty," I said to Cam as Mary Ellen stood by the table. "I never noticed that before."

"You got a problem with *that*, now?" he sneered.

"No, he doesn't," said Mary Ellen in my defense. "He's just being observant, right?"

"Right," I said. "Just like you." I wondered if she'd read the same book I had.

"That, my friend," said the hostess to Cam, "is a left-handed coffee cup."

Yep. We'd read the same book, all right. Hal Rosenbluth, the travel executive, had once written a story about a waitress who would size up her customers and then serve drinks to the left side of her lefty guests. It was a great lesson in adapting to the needs of customers and not expecting them to adapt to yours, and I hadn't thought about it for many years. It was cool to see someone actually putting it into practice.

Cam picked up the cup and gave it a dubious perusal. "Sorry. I don't see the difference."

"You've never heard of the left-handed cup factory?" asked Agnes.

"No. Can't say I have." Cam peered at her over the thick ceramic mug.

"There's a good reason for that," she said.

"Which is?"

"There isn't one, you silly young man."

We all had a good laugh at Cam's expense, which I have to admit, I very much enjoyed.

"I'll explain it to you later, southpaw," I said, patting his hand, and immediately regretting my patronizing tone.

Cam put the cup down and rolled his eyes toward the ceiling. Mary Ellen walked away, chuckling under her breath, while Agnes reached across the table and laid her delicate, veined hand on Cam's. "I'm sorry, Cam. That was very rude of us, but I assure you that it wasn't mean-spirited. Will you forgive us?" She went on to explain Rosenbluth's story. "That kind of observant, do it for the customer before they ask approach is just the way we do business here at The Wake-Up Call. I've done it that way my entire life. And that's ninety-plus years."

"But who's counting?" I chimed in.

"I am," she said. "Every blessed minute."

I let that sink in for a moment. "With respect, Agnes," I said. "There's clearly something very special about you and your diner."

"Thank you," she smiled.

"You're welcome, but that's not where I was going. For some reason, Edg sent me here to talk to you, but—and again I mean no disrespect—but why? I mean, I've eaten in a lot of great diners and restaurants but there's got to be something more to this; am I right?"

"Well, yes. There's always something more than what meets the naked eye, true?"

"True, but..." I was trying to think of a polite way to ask the question, but I was striking out. "To put it bluntly, Agnes, who are you and why are we here?"

Much to my relief, she laughed and said that she'd be happy to tackle the first part of the question. "But first things first," she said and waggled her fingers in the air to catch Mary Ellen's attention. She nodded at Agnes and then disappeared into the kitchen just as another server appeared at our table to refill our drinks. A few minutes later—it seemed like seconds, really—Mary Ellen returned with platters of sliced pastrami, roast beef, ham, and turkey, three kinds of cheese, French fries, onion rings, rolls, bread, condiments, potato salad, coleslaw and crisp, kosher dills. Cam and I stared in stunned silence.

"The Agnes special," Mary Ellen said with a smile. "Help yourselves, fellas."

Believe me, we did. As I assembled my first sandwich, Agnes began her story. And I enjoyed every blessed minute.

■ FORTY-TWO

Agnes Golden grew up in Chicago in a middle-class, black family who had high hopes that she would apply her terrific intellect and relentless drive to the practice of medicine. For as long as Agnes could remember, however, and to the shock and horror of her parents, she wanted to be a foodie. She wanted her own bar, restaurant, café, or even a hotdog stand on the pier at Lake Michigan. She wanted to make simple comfort food, serve it to fanatically loyal customers, and revel in the reputation that could only come through a truly inspired and mystical bowl of chili.

When she was in the fifth grade, she would fantasize about turning her family's home into a burger joint with very limited and exclusive seating and a celebrated reputation for the most sublime, and coveted, secret sauce in the city of Chicago. As she experimented in the kitchen she would imagine the crowds lining up along her street, waiting for hours with great anticipation for a precious seat at one of three tables set in the small living room.

That childhood fantasy stayed with her on some subtle, preconscious level all the way up through grade school, middle school, high school—where she was a star volleyball player,—college, and even through her first year of medical school. The pressure of being a female African-American med student in those days was significant, to say the least, and Agnes found her grades sliding down to average and her mind drifting more and more frequently back to her restaurant dreams.

She helped pay her way through school by waiting tables, which was no shock to anyone in her family, but when the excruciating time demands of med school forced her to choose between her restaurant job and poking at cadavers for a C average at best, she quit school. The irony of her quitting med school nearly causing her father a heart attack was not entirely lost on her. But it also didn't stop her from begging her dad for the money to finally start her own business and bring to fruition that small seed that so many of us leave buried in the soil of our childhood memories.

Agnes' Real Chicago Hot Dog and Chili Palace was born and the first menu-fliers printed on Agnes's 20th birthday. 31 years later, she sold her chain of 21 Palaces and, at the wheezy old age of 50-something, having achieved the rarified status of Chicago restaurant maven, moved to San Diego to retire.

She bought a big house in Del Mar overlooking the ocean and spent her days hanging out on the beach and learning to surf from some of the local legends, who became her second family.

"But old foodies never die," she said, picking a crisp onion ring from the wicker basket. "So I bought this little building and opened The Wake-Up Call so I could feed my friends and make a little money while I was at it. Just for fun, you know."

"Excuse me," said Cam. "Just so I'm clear on this. You're loaded, aren't you?"

I practically choked on my cheddar roll and for a panicked moment hoped that Dr. Heimlich was in the house.

"Cam!" I croaked. "What the...?"

"*What?*" he exclaimed. "I'm just asking a question. You *are*, right?"

"I've done very well. Yes, baby, I have done very, very well."

She was the embodiment of graciousness. As far as I was concerned. I'd have clobbered Cam with a cast iron skillet, if I were Agnes. Although I did have to give the boy points for focus, in that lovely story of Agnes' pursuit of her lifelong dream, all Cam saw was the payday. There could never be a drop of doubt that money was his prime boat floater.

■ FORTY-THREE

"It's all about the money for you, isn't it, Cam?" I said with rising vexation. "Isn't there anything else that turns you on? Anything?"

"Look," Cam said with an appetizing mouthful of coleslaw. "You're supposed to be helping me with my business, aren't you?"

I took a bite of my sandwich.

"Well, aren't you?" he persisted.

I turned to Agnes and explained the circumstances that had brought Cam and me together for the day, though I left out the details about the precariousness of Cam's employment situation. "Yeah, of course," I answered, setting my food back on the plate. "That's the general idea, sure."

"It's not the *general* idea; it's the *whole* idea. And business is about making money. That's it. No money, no profit, no business. Game over; end of story." He kept his eyes on mine but pointed a finger at Agnes. "This nice old lady here—no offense, Agnes—has obviously made tons of money. Don't even pretend that's not important, because it is. Jeez, Farber. It's almost like you think she should apologize for it."

"I'm just saying," I frothed, "that you should open up your freakin' eyes to other..."

With a surprising burst of energy, Agnes sat up and reached her hands across the table. Like a mother intervening in her children's sib spat, she grabbed each of us by the chin and pulled our faces toward her so we were both looking her in the eye. She didn't let go and—okay, I'll admit it—it started to hurt. I can't imagine what this scene must have looked like to the other customers, and when someone across the diner laughed, I was certain it was at us.

"Boys," Agnes said in a controlled voice. "It's time for you both to, and I mean this in the nicest way, shut the hell up." It was as though this gentle, innocent old lady had morphed before my eyes into a steely disciplinarian. Still clenching our chins in her sinewy fingers, she began, once again, to smile. She let go and gave each of us a pat on the cheek.

"May I speak?" It wasn't really a question. "Thank you. Cam is right, Steve. I'm proud of the money I've made over my lifetime. There is no point in starting a business, whether it's a restaurant, or a—what is it you do again?"

"I sell mortgages."

"Right, mortgages. Whether it's a restaurant, or a mortgage company, or a carpet cleaning operation, or a pharmaceutical company, the business has to make money. And the more the better, I say."

"Well, there you go," said a triumphant Cam with a wave of his fork. "That's what I'm saying."

"Steve?" She raised her eyebrows at me. "Care to chime in?"

"You just told me to shut the hell up, as I recall."

"Yes, I guess I did," she laughed. "So I guess I'll continue, then. Cam?"

"Agnes?"

"You're pretty successful, right?"

"I'm the best." The boy just oozed humility.

"Make a lot of money, do you, baby?"

"Never enough."

"Never enough," she repeated. "And where does your money come from?"

He took another bite of coleslaw. "Selling mortgages, like I said."

"Mmmm... hmmm," she mused. "And where would you guess mine comes from?"

"That's obvious. Selling food."

"I want you to look around this diner," she said gesturing her hand at the room. "And tell me what you see."

"I see people having lunch."

Agnes eyed him. "Oh, come on now, sugar. Tell me what you *see*."

He slowed his glance around the room slightly. "OK, there are people talking and laughing and eating and there are waitresses doing the same."

"And how many tables are empty?"

Cam craned his neck around. "Well, none, that I can see."

"That's right. Not an empty table in the house, and there rarely is. Do you know why?"

He shrugged matter-of-factly. "Food's good."

"Thank you. Anything else?"

"Price is right."

"And?"

Cam's face betrayed that he was drawing a blank.

"Does it look like people are enjoying themselves, Cam?" Agnes prompted.

"Yeah, I guess."

"How about all those people waiting outside?"

"What about them?" I finally chimed in.

"Do they look miserable?" She didn't wait for an answer. "No! They look happy, don't they?"

It was true. Everyone—whether eating at a table, waiting for food, or standing in line—seemed genuinely cheerful. It was kind of odd, now that I'd noticed it. Odd in a wonderful way.

"I'm going to tell you why they're happy, Cam. I'm going to tell you why, since the day I opened my first Hot Dog Palace, people keep coming back and spending their money with me and mine. I'm going to tell you why, Cam, but you're not going to believe me."

"Try me," he said in a patient, almost patronizing, tone.

"It's because I love them," whispered Agnes.

■ FORTY-FOUR

I'd heard this theme before from Pops, of course. I'd been struggling with his mantra, "Do what you love in the service of people who love what you do," and trying to put it into practice in my own life and business. So it was a little jarring when I heard what Agnes said next:

"This is how you stoke the fires of your success, Cam, by doing what you love in the service of people you love, who, in turn, love what you do for them."

"Uh-huh," muttered Cam. "So you're honestly telling me that you love every single individual human being that ever stepped into one of your restaurants for the last seventy-some-odd years."

I thought he laid out the challenge quite well, actually. That's exactly the thing that I was wrestling with, too. I sat up and leaned forward to hear Agnes' response.

"I wish I could tell you that," she said, folding her hands on the table. "I wish I could say that I have a heart big enough and a mind clear enough of judgment to embrace nothing but the goodness in every single person on this planet, saint and sinner alike. But I can't."

"So what *are* you saying then?" I asked before Cam had a chance to throw a barb.

"Well, it's really pretty straightforward, boys."

"That's not the word I was thinking," said Cam.

"Think what you will, honey, but it is really very practical. I may not have the capacity to love everyone, but I certainly do have the capacity to act as though I do and to run my business accordingly. And if I and my team can really do that, then no other business in my market space can come close to the experience that we give our customers."

Cam set his fork down. "Then explain something to me, please. How come I make so much money?"

Agnes tilted her head at him. "Why don't you tell me?"

"Yes, I will." He leaned back in the booth and laced his hands behind his head. "It's not lovey-dovey, I'll tell you that. I work my ass off; no one works harder than I do. In at 6:30am, out at 10:00pm most days. When I was a sales agent I'd make hundreds of calls, and if no leads were coming in, I'd go through the damn phone book, if I had to. My business is all about the transaction, the loan. I close the deal and someone else takes it from there. It's a numbers game and nothing else. And I've always generated more numbers than anybody."

"Wow, you have a great work ethic, to say the least," said Agnes with all sincerity. "And you must get a lot of referral business."

The comment stopped him for a moment and he shifted in his seat. "Nah. Don't need it."

Agnes paused. "And you're a manager, right?"

"Senior vice president of sales. Youngest of the execs," he beamed.

"That's something to be very proud of," she said, again, with total genuineness.

He was aglow, getting all warm and toasty inside as his ego expanded. "Yep."

"So, how about your sales team? Do they work as hard as you do?"

Cam grunted. "I wish. But I pump 'em pretty hard to get it all done."

"I'll bet you do, sugar. And they'd follow you through thick and thin, wouldn't they?"

Uh-oh, I thought. *Here it comes.* I had a feeling that Cam's balloon was about to go blammo.

Cam appeared to have divine intervention on his side because just then Mary Ellen stopped by to refill our drinks. She set her order pad on the table and whispered something in Agnes's ear. Agnes nodded, and Mary Ellen scurried away, leaving her order pad behind.

"She," said Agnes watching Mary Ellen, "is priceless. She helped me open this place and has been here ever since. Single mom, accomplished athlete, extraordinary businessperson. She runs the place now, but back when she was waiting tables, customers would wait in line just to get into her section. You know why?"

"She's fast?" said Cam, clearly happy to change the subject.

"I've seen faster, to tell the truth. In fact, sometimes she can be pretty slow turning tables over. So it's not because she's fast—but we were talking about you, weren't we? Oh yes, thick and thin, right? So how about it, Cam?"

Cam pretended not to know what she was asking. "How about what?"

"Why won't your team follow you?"

"I never said that." He was starting to smolder, and I was tempted to order a basket of popcorn to munch on while the fireworks went off.

"But it's true. I can tell by the way you're avoiding the question, baby. And also because you have to—how did you say it—pump them pretty hard to get results. They do what you tell them to do because you're the boss. They perform because they have to; not because they want to. In other words, Cam, you're not a leader at all; you're a taskmaster."

Cam bristled in his seat. "Wait a minute. Hold on. I'm not sitting around and barking orders while I'm relaxing under a coconut tree or something. I'm slammin' it harder than they are. I demand no more of them than what I demand of myself."

"Wrong!" Agnes erupted. "Wrong, wrong, wrong!" She slapped her palm on the table.

Everything stopped and heads turned in the diner. I was stunned to hear such thunder emit from this sweet old lady. When Mary Ellen looked back at us over her shoulder and shook her head as if to say *there she goes again*, however, I got the impression that an occasional Agnes cloudburst was to be expected.

"I want you to tell me right now why you work as hard as you do," she railed. "Tell me why you work those long hours, make all those calls, go to all those meetings, close all those loans. Tell me!"

Cam sat blown back in his seat with a startled expression on his face that I hadn't yet seen or even thought he was capable of making. His mouth was moving, but it took a moment for him to get any words out.

"It's my job," he sputtered. "It's how I get paid."

"And?" Agnes pressed.

"And it's a rush, it's a blast."

"And you love it," I said before I could stop myself. "You love the game, don't you Cam?"

"Yeah. Okay. Fine. There's nothing better," he said again with eyes rolling.

"Oh, yes there is," said Agnes, as if he were serious. "Yes there is, indeed."

■ FORTY-FIVE

It's funny how things work. As I look back on the trajectory of my own life, it seems to me that all the things I've done and all the people I've met have yielded lessons that have built on each other in increasingly meaningful ways. Some are convinced that the human experience is random and our time on this earth is not only infinitesimal but insignificant as well, the *life's-a-bitch-and-then-you-die* school of thought. I'm not much of a philosopher, so don't ask me to argue the finer points of this age-old debate between meaning and meaninglessness, but it sure looks to me as though life serves up one lesson after another, and, just when I think I've got it nailed, got it all figured out, I come to realize that I am, in fact, an idiot.

I had told Rich Delacroix that I like everybody. Sure, I'd been exaggerating a tad, but, compared to most people it was true. It takes a lot for me to dislike someone. Really, it does. I've had plenty of conflict, argument, and misunderstanding in my life, and some relationships that had started well ended badly. I've had a failed business partnership and a failed marriage, so I know what it feels like when someone lets you down and vice versa. Still, my shit list is very, very short. In fact, I pride myself on my ability to look into the eyes of another human being and find something in there to like, to appreciate, maybe even to embrace. That, I believed, is what made me a good leadership coach.

On that day, however, sitting across from that gem of a woman in her marvelous little diner, I realized just how far it was I had to go. She was starting to get tough on Cam, but she never gave the slightest hint, the faintest inkling that she was just tolerating or putting up with him as a favor to someone else. She invested herself completely in this little bag of wind just as I, to my dismay, was good and ready to write him off. *What does this say about me?* I was asking myself as Agnes was asking Cam an oddly similar question. The cloudburst had passed just as suddenly as it had begun.

"What would they say about you, Cam?"

"What would who say?"

"Well," she said, "let's start with your direct reports, your sales managers."

He poked his fork into a pickle. "Not a fair question. You'll have to ask them."

"All right, fair enough. But seeing as how they're not here, what do *you* say they'd say about you?" Again, the warmhearted smile to contrast my increasing need for Zantac. And believe me, it wasn't a food related need.

"They'd say I'm hard on them. They'd say I have no tolerance for laziness. Most of all, they'd say that I bring on the results."

"And your peers would say?"

"Okay," he fished his business card from his wallet and flicked it across the table. "Look at the title; that says it all, as far as I'm concerned."

She left it there without giving it the slightest glance. "And your customers?" Agnes asked patiently.

"What?"

"Your customers, Cam. Those people that bought you your car, what would they say about you?"

"How the hell am I supposed to know that? Listen, Agnes," he crunched the end of the pickle skewered on his fork, "I get my customers a rate that they're happy with and a program that'll give me the highest possible fees and commissions without hurting them. I do it fast and I do it right and that's the end of that. Everybody's satisfied. What else is there to know?"

"Okay, then!" she exclaimed and pushed herself up from the booth. I was amazed at her height: around six feet—a good inch or two taller than I am. She stood steady as a rock and looked down at us with hands on her hips. "Don't go away. I need to go talk with someone for a moment, but I'll be right back. I'll have Mary Ellen bring you some dessert, and when I return," she stared down at Cam, "It'll be your turn to listen to me. Got that, baby?"

She turned and was gone before Cam could respond.

■ FORTY-SIX

"And Judge Judy retires to consider her verdict," Cam smirked. He did that a lot.

"Listen, Cam," I began. "I promised Rich that I'd spend the day with you, get to know you a bit, but I gotta tell you..."

Mary Ellen, again with impeccable timing, swooped by, cleared the platters, and set in the middle of the table a plate with an outrageous, ginormous piece of chocolate cake. It had an inch-thick layer of glistening icing with a swirl jutting from the top as if it were flipping the bird to Dr. Atkins.

I picked up one of the two forks and sank it into the cake, helpless against the sweet siren song of the carbohydrates. "Oh, baby," I said; momentarily forgetting that Cam even existed. "This is worth the trip."

"You gotta tell me what?" Cam asked as he followed suit with his own fork.

"Hmmm?"

"You said, 'but I gotta tell ya...' You gotta tell me what?"

"I'm not sure this is going to work out, you and me."

"That's fine by me, Steve." He started to get up, but I grasped his wrist and motioned for him to stay.

"Look, Cam," I breathed. "We really need to try to get through the day. As much as I hate to say it, we both stand to gain something from this, especially you."

"Excuse me?"

"Bluntly, Cam? Your job depends on it."

"Is that a threat?" He fished for his cell. "Let's just call Rich right now and that'll be that."

Again, I grabbed his wrist. "Not a good idea. Trust me on that. Let's just give this thing another go, all right? I'm curious about what Agnes has to say, aren't you?"

Cam's wheels were turning and he looked a little shaken, as if he was beginning to realize that his situation might not be quite as rosy as he thought.

Then he did something that blew my mind right out its socket. It may very well have been the last thing I expected Cam to do at that moment.

He took out his WUP and began to write.

Fascination,
Gratitude, and Thou

■ FORTY-SEVEN

I tried to peer over Cam's shoulder, but he created a barrier with his arms as if blocking a cheating neighbor during a high school exam. I kept my mouth shut and let him scribble, which he was doing furiously. Suddenly I had the sense that someone was watching us and turned my head to see Agnes standing behind our booth, looking at Cam with a satisfied smile.

"Is that a Wake-Up Pad, baby?"

Cam jumped and turned his head as well. "Yeah, well, something to do while we were waiting for you." He slapped shut the notebook and started to stuff it back in his pocket.

"Keep it out, please, Cam," she said as she slid back into the booth. "You may want to take some notes." She turned her gaze to me and raised her eyebrows questioningly.

"Ummm... well... I haven't gotten around to picking one up yet," I told her. "I've got a tablet at home that'll do the trick, but I haven't been there since this morning."

She picked up Mary Ellen's order pad, which had been sitting at the end of the table. "Here, use this."

"But that's..."

"Just take it." She pushed it to me across the linoleum tabletop.

It was fresh and unmarked and as I flipped through the glue-bound pages, it was clear that this was not your typical server tool. The first half of the pad had the words *Scan & Eavesdrop* printed along the top of each page, followed by several pages with the heading *Ponder*. Farther back, another series said *Talking Points*, and the leaves in the final section each carried the heading of *Try This*.

"That's Mary Ellen's own design," said Agnes. "And it has to do with one of the many reasons that young woman is so extraordinary. Mary Ellen makes it her solemn mission to get to know—I mean really know—everyone who sits in her section. To the point where," she tapped on Cam's hand, "she'll know what side to serve the coffee on.

"She doesn't always succeed, mind you, and it does take her longer to turn over a table, but you know what happens? Her customers love her so much that they come back again and again, and will keep coming back as long as Mary Ellen is alive and well and working at The Wake-Up Call."

"So where does the pad come in?" I asked, flipping, once again, through the pages.

"Simple, really," Agnes beamed as though bragging about a favorite daughter. "She doesn't have to write orders, carries it all in her head. So, instead, she treats every customer encounter as an exercise in fascination. They think she's writing down their orders, but she's really capturing little gems of conversation and behavior—little nuggets of humanity. She may look like she's just waitressing or hostessing, but she's not."

Cam was clearly trying to get his mind around this. "Then what is she doing?"

"She's pursuing the Radical Edge, sweetheart. Her WUP is just the tool to get her there and keep her there."

"And there is where, exactly?" I asked, trying to recall what Edg had said in his letter.

"The Radical Edge is that zone of total value, total *significance* to one's self and to others. It's about achieving the simultaneous fulfillment of three of life's seemingly incompatible spheres."

Something had shifted in Agnes's tone. I was getting a glimpse behind Oz's curtain and seeing Her Wizardness for what she really was. Sure, she was a successful entrepreneur; sure, she was a kind though stern motherly figure but above all, I now saw, she was a philosopher who thought very deeply about things and took those thoughts very seriously.

"Your business, your personal life, and your effect on the world," she said. "When you're hitting on those three cylinders simultaneously, you've achieved the Radical Edge and life takes on an entirely new level of meaning."

"Smitty gave us a tutorial on WUPing this morning, but I think you've just put it in context for me," I said, stroking my chin in a scholarly manner. It's the only scholarly manner I have, come to think of it.

"Oh, yes, well, Smitty... Smitty is a WUP master," she chuckled at her description. "But that's not exactly a coincidence, my friends," said Agnes. She leaned in with a conspiratorial twinkle in her eyes. "I'm the one that started Billy Maritime down this road many, many years ago, and Billy taught it to Smitty when he was just a young pup like you, Cam."

Excuse me? "You taught this to Pops?" I don't know why I was stunned, but I was. "How did that happen? I mean, how were you two connected? You know what I mean." I was all but stammering.

"It was nothing formal, Steve. At first, he was my customer. He'd come in here with little Theodore—sorry, Edg—and our friendship just developed over the years. We did a lot of talking, that's all. Do enough talking, for enough years, and you're bound to not only learn from each other, but also help each other out along the way. He was the real genius; I just kind of goosed him along." She paused for a moment, obviously lost in reverie, and then let out a deep, trembling sigh. "Don't ever let anyone tell you that customers are just customers. If that'd been my attitude, I'd have missed out on one of my life's greatest treasures: Billy 'Pops' Maritime and his little boy, Edg."

I don't know if she'd meant to, but Agnes had baited the hook, tossed it into the pond, and jerked the line with perfect finesse. Cam was snagged. For him, merely mentioning the Maritime name made Agnes ripple with credibility; the fact that she knew Pops so well made her virtually irresistible. That's pretty much how I felt, too.

Agnes snapped back to the present. "But you're not here to talk about the Family Maritime, are you?"

"Works for me!" I exclaimed.

"Some other time, Steve." She responded looking at Cam, who met her eyes with full attention, pen at the ready in his left hand. That was a first, and it was clear that Agnes was going to take full advantage.

"Stoke your business, amp your life, and change the world—a modest promise, to be sure," she said with obvious understatement. "We'll take them one at a time, starting with business, okay?"

"That's what it's all about for me," Cam responded. "Chuck the other two, far as I'm concerned."

"Well, now that's just the problem, isn't it, Mr. Summerfield? You're not concerned far enough."

■ FORTY–EIGHT

In retrospect, I should have seen it coming, and if I'd known what was going on back at ILGI at that very moment, I'd probably have patted Cam on the head and said goodbye right then and there.

It's been called a lot of things throughout history: mutiny, uprising, revolt—insurgency is a popular one these days—but whatever colorful descriptor you choose, that's what was going down in the richly paneled office of Rich Delacroix.

He stood at the floor to ceiling window and looked down at the Mormon temple and at the highway beyond, wistfully picturing himself behind the wheel of his Mercedes Roadster. With the blue sky above and a V12 under the hood, he could rocket north toward San Francisco and soon be far away from the sudden, choking tension that had gathered in his office like a thunderhead. He could, that is, if it weren't for those three irritating letters that followed his name on the door: CEO.

Rich turned to face the six sales managers who comprised the entire team of Cam's direct reports. These were the folks responsible for the sales agents and Cam, in turn, was responsible for them, which, it should be obvious by now, was precisely the problem.

Lisa Appleman, a petite, crisply professional woman in her late 20s, spoke up first.

"There's a rumor going around the floor," she said, getting right down to business, "that you're going to put Cam back on the phones, and that he won't be in management anymore, or something to that effect."

Rich sighed. Few things are more disconcerting than a leak in the executive team. He was going to have to figure out where the fissure was, but he couldn't think about that right now. Not with six pairs of eyebrows raised at him in anticipation. *Neither confirm nor deny*, Rich thought. He really hated politics but he also knew he had to handle this with more than a dollop of finesse. Whether they wanted him to or not, he certainly wasn't going to preside over a kangaroo court. Yet, these managers and their sales agents were the best in the business and the backbone of his company, so he damn well better listen to what they had to say on the contentious subject of Mr. Cameron Summerfield, SVP.

"Okay," said Rich. "Everybody have a seat and let's talk this through." They all sat on the sectional leather couches at the far end of the office and Rich continued.

"What have you heard, and what do you want to know?"

"First of all, is it true? Is Cam being demoted?" asked Sergio Velasquez, a manager who had been at ILGI about six months longer than Cam. He had watched Cam come on board, catch fire, and scorch right past him on the corporate highway. The day Cam became big boss man was the worst day of Sergio's professional life—not that he was one to hold a grudge or anything. "Because," he went on without waiting for an answer, "we think it would be better if you fired him altogether." Not that he held a grudge or anything.

"We?" exclaimed Lisa. "Speak for yourself, okay? That's insane. Cam's the best salesman any of us have ever seen. I'll take him on my team, Rich, and we'll kick your butt, Serge," she challenged with a grin.

"Fine, take him," said Sergio with a dismissive wave of his hand. "Just keep him and his smug, holier-than-thou attitude the hell away from me and my guys."

"Excuse me; may I say something?" said Rich with exaggerated calmness, a valiant attempt to overcome the pressure pulsating in his cranium. "What to do about Cam—if anything—is not your decision," his eyes moved back and forth between Lisa and Sergio. "It's mine. I do want to hear what you have to say, but the decision is ultimately mine and mine only. Everybody understand?"

All heads nodded, but only Sergio's tongue wagged. "Rich," he said with strained patience. "With all due respect, we're the ones who have to work with him day in and day out. We're the ones who have to clean up the messes he makes when he freaks out, intimidates, or even runs off someone on our team, and we're the ones who have to make sure that our agents are bringing in the numbers in spite of Cam's leadership, not because of it. So, of course you're the one who has to decide what to do, we get that, but there's something you need to get, too."

Rich stared at Sergio with raised eyebrows. "Which is?"

"If you make the wrong decision, you'll kill this management team."

■ FORTY-NINE

Agnes sat up and smoothed her sweater. "Let's start with the obvious: we're all businesspeople here, agreed? And can we all agree that we'd have no business without customers?"

We nodded.

"Okay; Business 101 completed, so let's move on. You boys better finish that cake, this is the one school where eating in class is required."

We obliged.

Agnes waved her hand. "I'm not going to rehash all the conventional customer service wisdom. If you don't know those things by now, then there's nothing I can do for you. Process is important; CRM technology, customer-focused strategies, complaint handling skills: all important. We can all get better at those things, to be sure. Right, sugar?"

"Yeah. I guess so, sure," said Cam, but without his trademark flippancy.

"But," she continued, "If you really want to stoke your business till it burns so bright that everyone will take notice, there are two things you must be with complete abandon." She paused and looked expectantly at each of us. "You may want to write these down."

That was obviously not just a friendly suggestion so I clicked the button on my pen.

"Hold on," Cam said. "That doesn't sound right. Don't you mean two things we have to *do*?"

"I most certainly do not," she replied firmly. "There are thousands of things to do, I'm not even going to pretend I know what they all are, but all those things will come from the two things to *be*. And they are," she forged ahead, "One: be deeply fascinated by the life of every person—customer, employee, colleague—your business touches; and two: be deeply grateful for who they are and what they do."

Cam squirmed but said nothing.

"Too flowery? Too girly? If there's one thing you should have gathered about me by now, boys, it's that I am certainly not made of sugar and molasses. I'll kick your ass from here to Hialeah if I think it'll help you, so don't you *ever* accuse me of being fluffy." She glared at Cam.

"I didn't say anything," he whined.

"Umm-hmm," she looked at him askance. "It all starts with the *heart*, Cam. If you develop a sincere love for people, you'll automatically be fascinated with and grateful for them. If you're fascinated with them, you'll discover how to add value to their lives. If you're genuinely grateful for their patronage, partnership, or friendship, you'll show them in ways that are sincere and meaningful. Those are the essential elements of a fabulously productive business relationship, or any relationship, for that matter."

This was familiar territory for me. "Pops called it 'do what you love in the service of people who love what you do.'"

She pointed to a small sign hanging on the wall behind the counter. I squinted at it, but the writing was too small for me to read.

"Pops and I kicked that around for years. He finally crafted the words just so, and it became his mantra. He taught it to anyone who cared enough to listen, which many did, of course, but there were only a few who really got it in their bones, you know? Edg has it, for example, and so does that lovely clown, Smitty. And maybe the both of you will, too." She zeroed in on Cam. "Is this making sense to you?"

"Whatever you say," he muttered.

"What?" I said, picking up his uneasiness with my refined sense of the obvious.

"This sounds like personal stuff, not business wisdom," he oozed.

"Well, baby," Agnes sighed, "contrary to what the old school bureaucrats would have you think, business is a deeply personal endeavor. Whether you intend to or not, you put your stamp on every bit of work you do, and you leave an indelible impression on every customer and colleague you touch. Each one of those impressions speaks volumes of truth about who you are. Business is not a mask; it doesn't hide your face. It unveils it, wrinkles, moles, warts, and all."

"I don't think so," said Cam starting, again, to fidget in his seat. "Work is work; personal is personal. Who I am at home and what I do there is nobody's business but my own."

"I'm not saying you should shower with your team, Cam," Agnes jabbed. "When you go to the bathroom, I'd much prefer that you close and lock the door, believe you me. Certainly, there are always lines of appropriateness, and each of us has to determine where to draw those lines. What is vital to understand, however, is that you can hide some of the things you do, but you can't hide who you are. And you shouldn't try to because your uniqueness is what sets you apart. I defy you to show me another Cam Summerfield anywhere on this planet."

God forbid, I thought to myself behind the bathroom door, as it were.

"That old saying, *it's not personal; it's business* is just plain false. Business *is* personal, personal, personal," she tapped three times on the linoleum tabletop for emphasis. "And," she twinkled, "is there anything in the human experience more personal than love?"

I regarded that as a rhetorical question.

"Love is your leverage," Agnes said. "And if you're observant, if you stay fascinated and grateful, love will hand you your competitive advantage on a solid gold platter." She rested her fingers on Cam's Wake-Up Pad. "This pad will only help you if you use it with your heart."

"Okay," huffed Cam. "Now we're getting a little too, like, *feel the force, Luke*. It's a *notebook*, Agnes, not a freakin' light saber."

"It's not magic, baby. There is, in fact, nothing more real and practical than applying love to the work you do."

"All right, then," Cam challenged. "Show me."

"I have been," she smiled, pointing to the front of the diner. "Since the minute you walked through those doors."

■ FIFTY

"You fascinate me, Cam," Agnes cooed.

"Excuse me?"

"You heard me, *fascinate*. That's why I've been spending all this time with you. I love to discover things about people; and in that act of discovery I can oftentimes—not always, but often enough—figure out how to help. And if I can do that, I've earned a customer, a partner, or a treasured friend for life."

She turned to me. "And as Cam and I have more time together, which I certainly hope we will, I'll learn about him, about his life story, about the experiences that have made him what he is today. Doesn't that sound like a great deal of fun, Steve? Do you see how rich and rewarding that will be?"

Now it was my turn to squirm.

"What am I," said Cam with obvious discomfort, "a gorilla in the mist? What if I don't want to, as we say here in California, *share* any of that with you?"

"That's okay, sugar. I'll still learn about you by trying, but if you shut me out, that's your prerogative. Most people, though, will blossom under the attention. Let's take your sales department, for example."

"Yeah?"

"You're supposed to be their leader, right?"

"Supposed to be and am, yeah."

"All right then," she probed, "tell me one story about one accomplishment by one member of your team. Just one."

"All right, I will," he said trying to rise to her challenge. "Sue Proctor, a sales agent on this guy Sergio's team. She blew her quota away last month, after two consecutive months of probation. I didn't think she'd make it, but she did."

"How'd she do it?" I asked, not exactly fascinated, I admit, but certainly interested.

"Bottom line? She made a lot more calls and put in a bunch more hours. I think she worked on Sundays, too."

"You think?"

"No, I know. She worked on Sundays."

"That's it?" asked Agnes.

"What do you mean?"

"That's her story?"

"Yep."

"Tell me what you know about her."

"She's been working at ILGI for two years; before that she was a headhunter at a local boutique placement firm."

"That's not her story; that's her résumé," said Agnes. "Is that all you've got?"

"Look," Cam's voice rose slightly. "I don't have the time or the desire to..."

"Time is not the problem, Cam," Agnes cut in. "Desire is. You don't have it. You're not fascinated with Sue or, I'm guessing, anyone else in your department. True or false?"

Cam shook his head. "I'm deeply interested in their results, Agnes, that's my job. Once the results stop, so do I. We all say so long and that's that. Not everyone's cut out for this business, and if they're not, I'm not going to waste my time or the company's money coddling them."

"I agree with you, Cam, and I think Steve would, too." I nodded.

"But that's not the issue," Agnes said, lowering her voice to an emphatic whisper. "The problem is when your *superstars'* results suffer and they leave because of you— because they just can't stand working with you any longer. Or, just as bad, when people who could be superstars are never given the chance to blossom, to experience their own potential."

Harsh, but right on the money. That was the situation according to Rich, and it was precisely the reason he wanted me to work with Cam. I marveled at how Agnes was able to be so blunt without expressing the slightest hint of rancor.

"You said earlier," she rolled along without giving Cam a chance to react, "that your demands of yourself and your team are identical, but they're not. You're fascinated with yourself; you know what makes you tick, you know your own dreams, hopes, and aspirations and you do what it takes to achieve those things, right?"

Cam crossed his arms and sat back confidently. "Of course, I do."

"And that's why you've broken all the sales records."

He nodded. "Yes. I expect nothing less of myself."

"But getting *others* to break records is your job as a leader. In order to do that, you need to focus on *their* needs—*their* desires for *their* lives—and then show them how their performance at work will bring those things to fruition. You obviously don't, because you can't tell me one meaningful thing about any one of them. That's not only a lack of fascination on your part, baby; it's out-and-out contempt."

"Isn't that a bit much, Agnes?" I asked, surprised to find myself momentarily in Cam's corner. "That doesn't feel like contempt to me."

"Maybe not," she said. "But I'll guarantee you one thing."

"What's that?"

"It does to them."

■ FIFTY-ONE

"I know what you mean, Agnes," I said, and then turned to Cam. "Let me give you a perfect example of what she's talking about."

The best Extreme Leader that I'd met in my years of doing this work was a midlevel vice president at a formidable national bank. When I first met him, Dick was running the check processing operation in the bank's corporate facility. It was the closest thing a bank has to a manufacturing operation and it had an ethnically diverse, primarily blue-collar employee base. Showing me around the facility, Dick beamed with pride and enthusiasm as he regaled me with story after story of unprecedented productivity increases and skyrocketing employee morale.

It occurred to me as we talked that Dick rarely used the pronoun, "I," as in, "I've done this; I've accomplished that." In fact, the word "we" didn't come up that often either; instead, he told me story after story about individual people and how they'd risen to conquer one enormous challenge after another—and he told many of those stories with the hero standing right there. Some appeared embarrassed by the spotlight, but every one of them, without exception, expressed some variation of a glowing "thank you" before scurrying back to work.

It's not as though Dick didn't have an ego. He could puff out his chest along with the best of them, but he saved that for the appropriate time, usually after dinner and more than a few drinks, and always tempered his boasting with a good shot or two of self-deprecation. Moreover, he always brought it back to one central theme: his deep gratitude for his employees' spunk, imagination, personalities, and drive. I remember getting the distinct impression that he was in awe of their accomplishments. In retrospect, I could see that he was, indeed—to use the word of the hour—fascinated with them.

Simply put, Dick loved the individuals on his team, even the ones he eventually had to let go.

Several years later, after his promotion to senior vice president—which was essentially deity status at the bank—surviving a merger, and moving to another division, Dick was charged with conducting what some euphemistically call a reduction in force. Over a 12-month period, he culled his division from 1,500 people down to 175, mostly through outsourcing. During that same period, however, employee satisfaction percentages went from the mid 70s to the high 80s, raising steadily all throughout the process. That was counterintuitive. And it wasn't because the survivors were happy to still have a job—which they were—but anyone who's ever been through a layoff will tell you that the event is usually characterized by increased stress, cynicism, and even paranoia. That was not the case in Dick's domain.

When I asked him how he accounted for the amazing spirit and morale even as people were jetting out the door, he said, "Two things: I kept everyone involved and I continued to let them know I cared, every freakin' day."

Although, to be fair, being the potty mouth that he was, Dick's language was a bit earthier—a bit more colorful.

He didn't say freakin'.

Maybe that's part of the reason they loved him right back.

GET MY REWARD

6

■ F I F T Y – T W O

"Your friend Dick is a storyteller," said Agnes, "because he loves the subject of his stories, and his desire to share their stories is how he shows his gratitude. More important, though, is that in learning their stories, he can adjust his approach and create the environment that will be the most productive for his team. That's the raw material for stoking your business."

"That guy didn't use a WUP, though, did he, Farber?" Cam allowed a small smile to cross his face.

"Never heard of it, I'm sure, Cam," I said. "But he'd have been all over it if he had." I was taking my own mental inventory of how much I really knew about my customers and colleagues, and I was coming up painfully short. I knew the basics, sure. After all, I had just told a story about Dick, but my knowledge of others didn't really run very deep at all. If Mary Ellen was able to do it on a glorified order pad, then I was sure I could, too.

"Well, then," Agnes said as she pushed herself up from the table. "That's a pretty good start for today, don't you think?"

"Start?" exclaimed Cam.

"Put it this way, sugar," she said as she looked around the diner. "Your fascination with others gives you the raw material to focus on and wrap your business around your customers and employees. Your gratitude keeps them engaged and coming back, but if that's all you do in your time on this earth, it will have been wasted time, to be sure. There are two more elements of the Radical Edge, remember?"

"Amp your life and change the world," I proclaimed, ever the alert student. Actually, I had written it in my WUP on one of the "Eavesdrop" pages, but given the situation, I didn't consider that cheating.

"Gotta have all three, boys. Gotta have all three." She turned to walk away and then paused and looked back at us. "By the way," she said as if she'd just remembered, "Your check has been taken care of by a friend of yours."

"Really? Who? Smitty?" I guessed.

"It doesn't really matter, does it, Steve? But be sure to show your gratitude to Mary Ellen with a nice, fat tip." She winked at Cam and as she shuffled toward the front door she looked back over her shoulder one more time.

"See you tonight," she called. "And don't you dare be late."

Tonight?

Tuning In

■ FIFTY-THREE

This kind of thing shouldn't scare me anymore, but when I opened the door to my apartment and Smitty jumped out from the kitchen shouting an enthused *Hey there, buddy!* I nearly spat my heart right out of my mouth. *Definitely time to change the security code*, I thought as my eyes settled back in my head. He was drinking a glass of orange juice, which scared me, too, because I really couldn't remember buying it.

"Hope you brought that with you, Smitty, because if it came from my fridge, I can't vouch for its safety."

"Aged to perfection," he said, patting his stomach. "And guts of titanium."

"And to what do I owe this wonderful surprise? You get lost on your way to Nordstrom?" He was wearing a tie-dyed tank I figured had around the same purchase date as that orange juice.

"Just being the messenger, once again, my wry pal-o-meeno." He handed me a piece of paper with driving directions scrawled on it in thick pencil.

When Cam and I were leaving the diner, Mary Ellen had intercepted us and said she'd be calling me with directions to Agnes's house in Del Mar.

"Dinner is at 6:30," she said. "But Agnes usually turns in early, so don't plan on staying very long. And she drinks red, so you may want to bring a bottle of cab."

I don't know if Cam had mastered the look of incredulity before today, but he sure had it down now.

"I never said I was available for dinner," he'd said. "I've got plans tonight, so I'll have to pass."

Mary Ellen looked at me as if to say, *take care of it, please*, and hurried off to tend to a customer. So, I did. After cajoling Cam all the way back to the car, I'd finally gotten him to commit to one hour at Agnes's place. I'd closed the deal by offering to bring the wine, and we drove in blessed silence back to Mission Beach where he'd left his car last year—I mean earlier that morning.

"This is how Mary Ellen calls?" I said to Smitty. This guy was like a walking telegram. "Is this your new job, Western Union man?"

"I yam what I yam and I do what I do; if'n you don't like it then shame on you." He howled with laughter, having charmed the stuffing out of himself with his little rhyme. "So..." he wiggled his eyebrows above his tinted glasses, "... how'd it go with little Cammie and Agnes the Magnificent?"

I wanted to say that I was hoping Cam would get stuck on the railroad tracks and run over by the Amtrak Coaster, but I was too nice to say that out loud. I didn't really mean it either, that would be way too troublesome for all those innocent passengers.

"We'll see about Cam," I told him. "Just when I think something is sinking into that concrete cranium of his he says or does something to really tweak my gizzards." I stopped for a moment, fished my WUP out of my shirt pocket, and wrote tweak my gizzards. I don't know why, just a spontaneous impulse, I guess. And I was trying to get myself in the habit of WUPing.

"But Agnes," I went on, "really is magnificent. I've never met anyone like her. I can't wait to spend more time just soaking up her perspective on things."

"Well, I sure wish I could be there with you for dinner at her house tonight," said Smitty. "I was invited, ya know," he insisted, catching my expression, "but I convinced her that it'd be better if I wasn't present and accounted for this evening."

"Why's that?"

"Just a feeling, that's all."

"What kind of feeling?" I asked with a subtle, growing sense of foreboding.

"Well, I think there's a storm comin' in, so I wanna be home where it's nice and cozy."

A storm in San Diego is newsworthy, but I hadn't heard anything about it and said so to Smitty.

"Not that kind of storm, you ninny."

"What do you mean? What other kind is there?"

He shot me a roguish grin. "A shit storm."

■ FIFTY-FOUR

I drove the winding road up the cliff overlooking the deepening Pacific and took in the ridiculously beautiful view. The sun was heading down in the sky as I was driving up the road toward Agnes's house. I was more than a little curious about what kind of place I would find. Agnes struck me as simple and unpretentious, and I expected her house to be the same. I pictured a small, comfortable, one-story with a shingled roof and a neatly manicured wedge of grass out front. Maybe a little porch with a swing and a planter full of geraniums. That's why I soon found myself checking and rechecking the address on the page and comparing it with the plaque on the tall iron gate at the end of the street. There was no denying it, the number was the same, so I drove up and pressed the intercom button.

A moment later, the gate rolled aside and I eased up the driveway, lined on each side with enormous Canary Palms, the kind whose immense height and breadth and majestic quality always takes my breath away. If one of those massive fronds were ever to fall and hit you on the head, you'd be skewered to the earth like a shrimp on a spit.

I pulled into the driveway, paced up the steps to an oversized stained glass and hardwood door, and rang the bell, though I didn't need to. Before I could even take my finger off the button, the door swung open and Mary Ellen stood there, beaming.

And I mean beaming—as in radiant—as in hamma, hamma, hamma. She was dressed in a classy, black, designer evening gown with a string of black pearls swooping down her neck above a plunging V.

"Hamma, hamma, hamma," I actually said, ever the eloquent Casanova. "You look... you look..."

"Thank you," she laughed, mercifully letting me off the hook. "C'mon, follow me."

Not... a... problem. She took me down a hallway, which was like a celebrity photo gallery. Here was a young Agnes posing with the late, original Mayor Daley of Chicago machine notoriety; Agnes and the late Chicago columnist, Mike Royko, who was the perpetual thorn in Daley's side; Agnes with Oprah, with Clinton, with Reagan, with Jim Belushi and Dan Ackroyd, with Jesse Jackson, and,—I almost passed out when I saw this one—a group shot with Agnes and every single scrawny and fantastic member of The Rolling Stones.

I dragged my chin along the floor down the hall and into the living room. The sun was settling down over the horizon and casting a red and orange glow on the surface of the sea. I knew this because I was looking at it through the panoramic window that arched around the round living room in which we now stood. The furniture was comfortable looking, very simple and classic so as not to attract attention to itself. Earth tones, greens, and muted purples created a warm, inviting environment that seemed to say, *come in, sit down, stay as long as you like.*

Ever the waitress, apparently, Mary Ellen took the two bottles of Silver Oak Cabernet that I'd brought and excused herself saying she still had some things to do in the kitchen. I walked up to the window and looked out at the breaking waves, way down at the bottom of the cliff.

"Do you like the view?" Agnes walked up behind me and put her hand on my back. I turned and gave her a hug and didn't bother to answer the question, not verbally, anyway. She gestured for me to follow her into a large but informal dining room, also with a spectacular view, and we sat down together at the table which was, I noticed, set for four.

"Cam should be here any second," I said after several minutes of my effusive praise for Agnes's amazing home. I nodded at the extra place. "Who else is joining us?"

The doorbell chimed and moments later Mary Ellen brought Cam in to join us at the table and then returned to the kitchen where we could hear her clinking dishes and clattering pans. We exchanged polite hellos and small talk until Mary Ellen emerged carrying four plates of endive and walnut salad in her experienced hands. The way she was dressed, she looked more like the lady of the house than the kitchen help, so I wasn't entirely surprised when she sat down and joined us at the table.

Cam did look a little startled, however.

"Mary Ellen is not only my treasured employee," Agnes explained, "but my caretaker here at home and," she rushed, not wanting to dwell on *caretaker*, "the cofounding director, with me, of the Foundation for Women in Social Enterprise."

Impressive, I thought. "But what about your kids?" I asked Mary Ellen, assuming that she lived here with Agnes. "I thought you were a single mom."

"I am," she said. "But the kids don't live with me."

"With their dad?" I assumed.

She laughed. "Not exactly. My son's 30 and my daughter's 26, both out on their own and doing fine."

I gaped.

"I know," she said with a smile. "You don't have to say it. I look young. Good genes. But I make no secret of the fact that I'm 51 years old." She raised a glass of sparkling water in Cam's direction. "Old enough to be your mother."

He gave her a slow once-over. "Now, that would be a shame," he crooned.

A wave of nausea was not a good way for me to start dinner, so I hastily raised my wine glass in a toast and we all started in on our salads.

After a few mouthfuls, Cam gave an overly obvious gander at his watch and then looked impatiently in my direction as if to say, *better get this moving*. Not that I was all that eager to oblige him, but out of respect for Agnes's generosity with her time and wisdom, I tried to get the conversation started.

"So, Agnes," I said. "Is there a reason, other than sharing fine company and fabulous food, that you invited us here tonight?"

"Yeah, thank you," said Cam. "I don't mean to be rude, Agnes, but I do have to leave pretty soon. Is there a particular subject that you wanted to talk to us about?"

Maybe he really didn't mean to be rude—*maybe*—but he sounded like he was bracing himself for a classroom lecture from a billowing old windbag professor.

"Oh yes!" exclaimed Agnes. "The best subject of all, Cam."

"Okay. What is it?"

"You." She answered. "The subject on the table is you."

■ FIFTY-FIVE

"The second element of the Radical Edge is *amp your life*, remember?" she said, ignoring Cam's uneasy body language. "Have to have all three: business, life, and effect on the world, remember?" she asked again.

"Yeah, I remember," mumbled Cam.

"Well, if you're going to amplify your life, you'll have to first know who, exactly, you really are."

Agnes pushed herself up from the chair and walked over to a vintage looking radio perched on a shelf between the dining and living rooms. I had noticed it earlier with its oversized dials and jukebox era appearance. She clicked on the power and soft static hissed through the large grates of the radio's speaker.

"Hear that?" she asked.

"Just barely," I said. "But that's okay; it's just noise. You may want to adjust the antenna or the tuner..."

She cranked the volume up. "How about now?" she called.

"It's louder, yes, but..."

She cranked again as if she were channeling the spirit of Mick Jagger from that picture on the wall.

"Now?" she was shouting over the noise.

The three of us at the table all clamped our hands over our ears and looked incredulously at each other. Leaving the tuning dial right where it was, Agnes mercifully turned the volume back down to barely audible fuzz and stood by the radio smiling as if she'd just shared with us a glorious composition.

"What's the matter?" she asked. "You didn't like that music?"

"That was noise," Cam groused.

"So it was," she admitted, bemused. "Well, then. Let's try that again."

Leaving the volume where it was, she now fiddled slightly with the tuning knob until the static evaporated and *Take Five* by Dave Brubeck jumped from a clear, crisp station. "Oh... a little jazz," Agnes delighted. "Louder, please," she said to herself and swung up the volume once again. This time, I noticed, none of us did any ear clasping whatsoever.

"Too loud?" she asked again.

"No, it's all right," I said. "That's one of my favorites, but I don't know how well I'm going to be able to hear everyone talk if you leave the volume where it is."

She nodded, turned the level down to where it filled up the background but didn't encroach on our voices, and came back to her chair. Silently, she placed her napkin back on her lap and reclined lazily, staring at Cam and then me.

She waited, saying nothing. Neither did I, or Mary Ellen, or Cam. Brubeck continued to swing in and out of the sound of the surf from the ocean below.

"Get the point?" asked Agnes.

Mary Ellen took a sip of wine and set her glass down. "That's one of her favorite demonstrations," she said with a smile. "Just think about it for a second. Loud static is annoying; loud music that you enjoy is exhilarating."

"And," Agnes broke in, "it's the same for each of us. The first thing we have to do is find our frequency, find our station, the one that clearly expresses who we are at our core. Have you ever," she turned to me, "helped your clients to find, clarify, and articulate their values or operating principles?"

"Sure. It's pretty standard procedure nowadays," I said, slipping easily into consultant mode. "Right up there with the vision thing."

"And it's important work, to be sure," she acknowledged. "But there's a missing piece, usually, in that process. Do you know what it is, Cam?"

"I know what they showed me when I started working, a poster on the wall with a bunch of statements about ILGI's values. That's all I know about it. I don't think it's any big deal one way or another." Again, he looked at his watch.

"That's a nice timepiece," commented Agnes. "May I see it? No... take it off and hand it to me, please."

Cam popped the clasp on his Tag Heuer and dangled the watch over the table. Agnes took it in her cupped hands and admired the workmanship. "Very, very nice," she cooed and handed it to Mary Ellen, who abruptly jumped to her feet and jetted into the kitchen, taking Cam's bling hostage.

"Hey! What are you doing?" he cried as if she'd ripped off his pinky.

"Relax, sugar." Agnes patted his hand. "It's not going down the disposal; I'll give it back, I promise. I just don't like the competition.

"Now listen to me for two minutes, Cam." She laughed when he looked at his wrist and dropped his hand to his lap in frustration. "The core of your business is not your customer, it's not your product, it's not your numbers, it's not your company, and it's not your team. Do you know what it is?"

"I'll bet you're going to tell me, aren't you?"

She ignored the sarcasm. "It's you, Cam. You have no business, no money, and no *life* without yourself right at the center."

"That's obvious, Agnes."

"Yes, it should be. So answer me one simple, little question, baby, and I'll give you back your watch and let you go on your merry way. Fair enough?"

He nodded. "Sure. Okay."

"Who are you?"

He stared at her. "Is that a trick question?"

"Yes it is, but not in the way you think. The trick," she told him, "is not in how we answer the question; it's in our uncanny finesse in avoiding it altogether."

■ FIFTY-SIX

"I already told you who I am, this afternoon at the diner," protested Cam.

"No. You told me what you've done. I'm asking you who you are." She paused for a moment and then relented. "Okay," she said. "We'll come back to you—if you want your watch back, that is."

Just then, Mary Ellen returned from the kitchen with four elegant plates of petite filets, small, perfect lobster tails, and lemon rice pilaf. She refilled our wine glasses, settled back in her chair, and placed her napkin on her lap.

"What did I miss?" she lilted, clearly knowing.

"I think you'll go first," said Agnes. "If you don't mind."

"I'm game," Mary Ellen laughed. "What am I going first with?"

"I think you're supposed to answer the who are you question," I said cutting into my steak. "And I'm pretty sure we don't want to hear your biography," I guessed.

"I'm all about service," she said without hesitation. "Everything I do comes from my desire to add more than I take from my relationships. Service fuels the way I work and the way I live my personal life, and it's the basis for all my choices. It's how I decide how I'm going to invest my precious time on this earth."

She'd obviously thought this through before, and I was impressed with her conviction and clarity in the way she delivered it.

Agnes said, "I made Mary Ellen my business partner because of the way she served our customers from the very first minute she started at The Wake-Up Call. And she cofounded the foundation with me for the same reason: she wanted to serve the needs of young women who, in turn, want to serve their communities. She served her marriage up until the minute her late husband—God rest his gentle soul—passed from cancer, and she still serves her children even though they're no longer living under the same roof."

"And," said Mary Ellen, looking at Agnes with gratitude in her eyes, "I serve my mentor here as her caretaker, though it doesn't really look like she needs one, does she?"

They raised their glasses to each other and sipped. It was a touching toast to deep camaraderie and friendship which couldn't possibly have gone unnoticed by our boy, Cam.

"So service is one of your core values," I said, trying to put it into a familiar language.

"If you like," said Mary Ellen. "But I prefer to think of it as," she pointed to the radio, "my frequency. It took me a while to find it, to tune in, as it were. There are a lot of values I hold dear: respect, integrity, honesty, love, and family, to name a few. But, for me, it all plays on the radio station called service." She clearly delighted in the metaphor. "Every value that I... well... *value* rolls up into service: service is the way I show respect; integrity and honesty characterize the kind of service I give to others. And if I'm really serving from my heart, I see everyone as family, not just my genetic relatives. That's the way it works for me, and the moment I got clear on that, the moment I tuned in, I committed to it with all my being."

"She turned up the volume," added Agnes.

"You amped your life," I said, catching the thread.

"And simultaneously stoked my business. Look at my career at the diner. I'm the *boss*, for goodness sakes!" she exclaimed with delight and a charming hint of self-deprecation. "And the foundation is one way I'm trying to change the world. I don't know how much of that I could have accomplished if I hadn't gotten clear on my frequency."

Cam ate in silence, never taking his eyes off the plate. I was enjoying Mary Ellen's dissertation immensely, but I couldn't wait for Cam's turn which, I suspected, was coming next. I admit that I was looking forward to hearing him confront such a personal revelation.

"Now," said Agnes, just as I'd hoped. "What about you?"

I looked at Cam with near sadistic anticipation, practically licking my chops at the prospect of watching him try to tune in to his station.

"So?" she said again. "What about it, Steve?"

Cam's gaze shot suddenly up from his plate and over to me, and I felt myself recoil. First he looked surprised, then relieved, and then amused at this little turn of events.

Now who's the sadist? I mused.

"Okay, I think I can do this," I said, nervously rubbing my hands together. "I've done a lot of values clarification exercises with my clients over the years, and I think I've got it narrowed down to a few things that are really important to me, you know, values wise, but as far as my frequency, my one overriding value or principle goes, well, that I'm not too sure about, but I'll sure give it a try." I was blabbering.

"I'm, well, I'm a Capricorn, for starters." I laughed the worst kind of laugh, the kind where no one joins in. "Umm... okay... I... I value family too, just like Mary Ellen said. And integrity, of course, I mean, who doesn't, right?" They all looked at me while I verbally thrashed about. "But, really, I'm all about, well... *man*," I interrupted myself. "I'm surprised this is so hard."

"What's hard about it, sugar?" asked Agnes with genuine compassion for my predicament.

"Narrowing it down to just one thing; there's so much more to it than that. It reminds me of that character in the movie *City Slickers* who said the key was to find the one thing in your life. I always thought that was a little silly. Human beings are much more complicated than that."

"Yes, we are, but it's not about finding your frequency by ruling out everything else; on the contrary, it's about finding the frequency that includes all those other important values and ideals. The very act of trying to wrap it all together is what's really important because in order to do so, you have to get very clear on what you mean by each value and principle. You have to define them, think them through, understand them to their core, and evaluate your life against each one. The clearer you get, the closer you get to the frequency that pulsates through your life and characterizes who you really are. So, Steve, just try. Off the top of your head, now, answer me one question."

"Okay, I'll try,"

"What's most important to you in the way you live your life?"

"A lot of things are important," I said.

"Let's try that again," Agnes chuckled. "Say the first thing that comes to mind. What," she repeated, "is most important to you in the way you live your life?"

"Freedom," I said, almost without thinking. "For me, I guess, it's all about freedom."

I'd never thought about it that way before, and the word surprised me. What was most shocking about it, though, wasn't the spontaneity of my utterance, and it wasn't the forceful way the word flew out of my mouth. It was the joy I felt in the act of saying it.

And the sudden comprehension that it was true.

■ FIFTY-SEVEN

"Well," said Agnes. "That sounds just lovely. *Freedom.* Now what does that mean, Steve? Can you make that clearer for us? Can you turn it up a bit?"

"It's what I've always wanted for myself, I guess, and for others."

"In what way?" coaxed Mary Ellen.

"The freedom to say what I think. The freedom to spend my time doing the things that bring me joy. Freedom of creative expression, the freedom to love without judgment. I think that's accurate." I was thinking out loud. Freely, I might add. "I think that's why I'm pulled to the field of leadership development, to help others experience that sense of freedom that comes from accomplishing extraordinary things in life. I mean, unleashing the potential in others is really the act of liberation, isn't it? Freeing the human spirit?"

"Makes sense to me," said Mary Ellen, and Agnes nodded in agreement.

"Yeah," I admitted. "Makes sense to me, too."

"That's a terrific start, baby," encouraged Agnes. "Now, here's what I want you to do." She leaned forward, and so did I. "Where's your WUP?"

"My WUP?" I said, patting my pants pockets.

"Don't tell me you don't have one. I know you left the diner with my order pad, Steve," said Mary Ellen. "I saw you take it." She wagged her finger at me. "I don't miss much, you know."

A wave of guilt settled over my head like a soft cloud. "I left it at home, I think. I didn't know there was going to be a quiz."

My intention was not to be funny, but it sure got a guffaw out of Cam. "Yeah, neither did I," he said. I guess he didn't bring his, either.

"There's always a quiz," corrected Agnes in all seriousness. "That's why you have to carry it with you all the time. I want you to write freedom in your WUP the second you get home, and then spend at least thirty minutes writing down what the word means to you."

"And then do what I did when I first tuned in to service," added Mary Ellen. "Start to list all the ways you can think of to bring more freedom into your life and the lives of others. And then, if freedom really is your frequency, as you do more of those things, your energy will kick up to levels that you've never experienced before."

"And if it isn't the right one?"

"Start over," she said. "And keep going until you find the one that is."

"It could take a while," said Agnes. "From the time I was a little girl in Chicago, I knew I wanted to have a restaurant. I was positively in love with the idea. I went to med school to please my parents, but I could never shake the fantasy. When I finally opened my first Agnes's Real Chicago Hot Dog and Chili Palace, I thought I'd arrived. But it wasn't until a few years later when I was about your age, young Mr. Cam, that I finally got clear on and tuned into who I really was beyond the labels of chef, or entrepreneur."

"And who was that?" I asked.

"I was and am and evermore will be devoted to human growth. When I realized that, I devoted more and more time and energy to the education and development of each and every one of my employees. Now these were fry cooks, mind you: cooks and cashiers and sweepers and cleaners who all started at the minimum wage, but I sought out opportunities for them to take on more challenge and responsibility. My business started to grow as well, and my employees took management jobs in my new locations. They became businesspeople in their own right, and some went on to start places of their own.

"Everything I do—*everything*—is with the intention to bring out the full capacity of those around me. And that's how I continue to grow, too, and will until the day I shuffle off to that Hot Dog Palace in the sky."

"I'm only one of many examples of what Agnes is talking about," Mary Ellen said, resting her hand on Agnes's shoulder. "I am living evidence that this woman's growth frequency is not only crystal-clear; her volume is turned all the way up to ten."

"So amping your life on the growth frequency helped you to stoke your business, as well," I commented.

"And change the world. Don't forget about that, baby. But we'll get to that."

Cam cleared his throat and all heads swiveled to him. "Dinner was great; I wish I could stay for dessert, but," he tapped his naked wrist. "I gotta bolt. I'm sure you don't need to pawn my watch, ladies, so if I could have it back, please, I'll get out of your way and you all can continue with... ah... *group*, or whatever you call it."

"Not until you've earned it," Agnes sang. "A deal's a deal, sugar. I believe it's your turn to answer the question."

"You mean, who am I?"

"That's the one," I said, relieved that the focus had shifted to Cam.

"My name is Cam Summerfield. My rank is senior vice president. My employee number is 135. My *frequency* is impatience and my time is now up. Watch, please." He held out his hand.

I'm a pretty laid back, find-the-humor-in-the-situation kind of a guy. Most folks will tell you that I'm easygoing, quick to forgive, and slow to anger. But the people who know me well—my family, some close friends, for example—know something about me that others do not: I have a low aggravation threshold. When that threshold is crossed; when the dam is breached, if you prefer, it's not a pretty sight. I have been known to blow like Moby, and, although I don't see what the big deal is, I've been told that I scare the living hell out of those on the receiving end. Cam did not know this about me, nor did anyone else in our little dinner party. My new little buddy of the day, however, was dangerously close to igniting my inner Hulk. I felt a familiar, David Banner-like tremor building somewhere deep in my chest.

I think Agnes must have sensed something because she asked Mary Ellen to retrieve the watch and told Cam that she understood, and that it was just fine, sugar, it was a pleasure to have his company if even for a short while. It was hard to hear through the thunder raging in my ears, but that was the gist of it.

I breathed, took another breath, and said, "Just one moment, please."

Then I waited for Mary Ellen to sit back down before I continued. "Cam, if you've listened *at all* to *anything* that these wonderful women have shared with us this evening," I was really trying not to hiss, "then you know that they didn't invite us here for their own good. They're doing just fine, thank you very much."

So far, so calm. I paused for a gulp of water.

"Now, I've learned a lot tonight, and I'm very grateful for that," I felt myself calming a little. Gratitude will do that to you. "But we're here for your benefit, Cam. Don't you get that? They invited us here to help you, and I think it would be the honorable, right thing for you to try, at least.

"So," I spoke into his silence, "how about really trying to answer the question, okay? Cam? Would you do that, please?"

"Okay," he started sweetly enough, "How about this? How about it's none of your flippin' business who I am or what my *freeeeeeequency* is." He made his voice warble like the Outer Limits. "I've answered the damn question. I'm a moneymaker. I'm a hard worker. I've earned my stripes and that's all you need to know. You wanna know my story? Fine. Here it is: I grew up poor. When I was little, I slept in a drawer in my mother's bedroom. I fought my way through high school and swept floors at the 7-Eleven for money because I never had an allowance. Is that what you want to know? Boo-hoo, poor me. Is that what you want to hear?

"You wanna know my frequency, Agnes?" he snarled. "It's get mine. That's it. Nobody's gonna give it to me, so I'm going to get it myself. Okay, now?" he shouted. "Everybody happy? Is that *amped* enough for you?"

"Enough!" I shouted back. "You don't get it, do you, you ungrateful, self-centered little punk? Because of you, I got the chance to meet and learn from these remarkable people, and I'm glad for that, but you, Cam, are not worth another nanosecond of effort from me or anyone else.

That's... that's it for me; I'm done with you. I'll call Rich in the morning and tell him you're on your own. And good *flippin'* luck to you."

I got up and left to find the bathroom. I closed the door behind me and rested my forehead against it. I turned on the tap in the sink, splashed cold water on my face, and looked at myself in the mirror. Already the waves of regret and failure were rolling over me.

Here I was, supposed to be a leadership coach, but I couldn't find it in myself to work with this kid who undoubtedly needed help more than anyone I'd ever worked with before. What could I do, though? He didn't want it or he was just too proud to admit that he did. Either way, I had to let it go and chalk it up to experience. Maybe this failure would make me a better coach for others that I'd meet down the road.

What had I learned from this? That's another question to work out on my WUP, I figured. I dried my face on a soft, cotton towel embroidered with small, purple flowers, took a few more deep breaths, and headed back to the dining room.

Cam was gone, and Mary Ellen was clearing the table in silence.

"Feel better?" Agnes asked with a knitted brow.

"Well, that's that," I sighed as I sat and poured myself a cup of dark, rich coffee. "I really botched that one all to hell, didn't I?"

"If it makes you feel any better, baby," she said, "he did thank us for dinner before he left." Her laughter that followed did make me feel better.

The three of us moved to the living room and sat facing each other in soft, upholstered brown and green loveseats. I set my cup down on the coffee table and leaned back into the comforting little sofa. "I'm really sorry, ladies," I said. "That was totally unprofessional and uncalled for. I wish I could call a do-over."

"Don't worry about it, Steve," said Mary Ellen on behalf of the both of them. "We all lose it from time to time. I know I have."

"Oh, yes," agreed Agnes. "My blowouts make yours look like a delicate spring shower." They both had a good laugh at that from a shared history, no doubt.

"I was really impatient with him all day, you know? Tonight pushed me over the edge, but I was already teetering on it. What else could I have done?" I pleaded.

"Why are you so worried about it, sugar?"

"Isn't it obvious?" I said. "I'm supposed to help people like Cam, not chase them away."

"The modern malady, Steve, is people living lives of quiet desperation. The three of us here, and many others like us, the ones who want to use their gifts to change the world for the better, prefer to live lives of amplified exuberance. That's how we move mountains, baby. Cam isn't ready to look deep enough into himself to find that clear, inspiring voice. So, even though it's in there somewhere, he's got nothing to amplify. Not yet, anyway."

"Besides, what makes you think you didn't?" asked Mary Ellen.

"Didn't what?"

"Help him."

"Were we all at the same dinner?" I looked at each of them. "That was a complete, total, and utterly miserable failure."

They each looked at me.

"Wasn't it?" I said.

"No, baby, it wasn't," said Agnes the Wise. "You helped him more than you know. We all did."

The Reunion

■ FIFTY-EIGHT

I drove back to my apartment in silence. That may not sound strange given that I was by myself, but usually I've got the music cranked up—a little Stevie Ray or John Hiatt, maybe—and I'm yowling along like an auditioning *American Idol* contestant. I was thinking about Cam, of course, and trying to come to terms with the whole deal. Who knows? Maybe there was still hope for him.

As I crossed over the bridge to Mission Beach and saw the roller coaster lit up in all its urban glory, my thoughts, for some reason, turned to my daughter, Angelica. She was just about Cam's age, I realized with a start. When she was younger she, too, was leading a life of quiet desperation, as do many young teenagers who haven't yet discovered their own frequency.

In some ways, my daughter was different from her peers. Instead of fighting to get out of the house, as most teenagers do, Angelica preferred to stay in the family nest and take care of her younger brothers. At 14, she was a domestic, maternal, and altogether lovely child—and, I have to admit, it was great having a built-in babysitter under the same roof. As she approached her seventeenth birthday, however, she was still a homebody.

I know that many parents would kill to have their teenagers stay at home, but what troubled her mother and me was *why* Angelica stayed home. She was a paradox of confidence: at home she was queen of the roost and a paragon of responsibility to her brothers. Away from home, however, she was fearful as a finch outside its cage. We came to realize that we had far more confidence in Angelica's abilities than she had in her own, and that we needed to create a situation where Angelica could prove herself to herself.

So in the summer of Angelica's seventeenth year, we sent her away—far away. We sent her to Italy, by herself, for six weeks. On one level, she desperately wanted to take this trip; on another, she was terrified.

We found her a room in Florence and enrolled her in Italian language and fine art classes. Before she left, Angelica and her mother planned every minute of her travel schedule down to the finest detail: she would fly from San Francisco to New York's Kennedy airport, switch planes, and fly on to Milan. At the Milan airport she would catch a bus to the station in central Milan, get on a train, and ride another seven hours to her cousin's house. She would stay there and decompress for a few days before traveling up to Florence where her Italian living and studying adventure would finally begin.

You may think it extreme of us to send our daughter on such a potentially perilous journey. You'd be right in the conventional, suburban sense, I suppose, but we *knew* she could handle it. She only suspected she could.

On the day of her departure, watching her walk down the Jetway at SFO, I had a vicarious jolt of joy and liberation. I remembered the first time I'd gotten away from my father and set out on my own. "She's going to have the time of her life," I whispered to her mother. Before she stepped through the airplane door, Angelica turned and, with a tremulous half-smile on her face, waved goodbye. *She's going to have the time of her life*, I said to myself.

I didn't fully realize, however, that I would never see the same little girl again.

Several hours later, Angelica arrived in New York and, embracing the power of the phone card—remember those from the pre-cell days?—called home.

"I'm in New York and you didn't tell me I was going to have to switch terminals.—I had to take a bus!—and the flight to Milan is delayed and I'm at the gate and I'm okay and *I'm ready to come home now!*"

We calmed her down and reassured her that she really was okay, and that everything would be fine as soon as she got on the plane. The flight was delayed for five hours—we got the hourly update—and we gratefully breathed a sigh of relief when Angelica was finally winging her way to Milan. She landed several hours later, got off the plane and went directly to the nearest phone.

"I'm in Italy now and I'm going to catch the bus and I couldn't figure out how to use the phone and I think I know where the bus is and *I'm ready to come home now!*"

Again, we calmed her down. She found the bus, took it to the train station and again, one hour later, she called home:

"I'm at the train station now!"

Her mother and I, standing in our kitchen back in Marin County, California, felt like we were in the war room, like we should be moving a pin on a giant wall map and shouting she's made it to the train station! into the radio.

"And the schedules are different from what we thought and nobody speaks English and I found the right platform and *I'm ready to come home now!*"

I'm not exaggerating; I am quoting verbatim. We calmed her once again and seven hours later, from her cousin's house, guess what? She called.

"Now, *look*," she said to her mother. "I made it to New York, I made it to Milan, I made it to the train, and now I'm here. *And now I am ready to come home.*"

So I got on the phone and I said to her, "Listen, honey, I gotta tell you something: You're having the time of your life. You just don't know it yet."

To say that the person who came home six weeks later had had the time of her life would be a gross understatement. What she'd done, in fact, was created a new life entirely.

The next summer Angelica backpacked around Europe, and the summer after that she and her mother volunteered in a Guatemalan orphanage. She did her junior year of college in Madrid, Spain, and years later, when she was 23, she took a summer internship with the U.S. State Department at the American consulate in—who says life is random—Milan.

She was one of four interns accepted out of 5,000 applicants. And even though the Foreign Service was not, she was to discover, her cup of tea, she is now a bona fide woman of the world with a global perspective on life and the human condition.

To this day, I feel great about having helped her to discover more of her own capability. The truth of the matter is, though, all I did was give her a nudge; a nudge that she would have fought with her every fiber if she hadn't wanted it in the first place.

Cam was going to stay right where he was, I figured, because he didn't want it any other way.

Mission Boulevard was teeming with pedestrian traffic as I turned onto my street and pulled around back to the garage. I clicked the door opener and pulled in. The garage had been empty when I left, it always is, but there was something sitting right in the middle of the floor. I slammed on the brakes and jumped out to take a look.

It was a skateboard, and it wasn't mine, I knew, because I've never owned one. I always figured that it would be a lot easier simply to smash my knees with a sledgehammer. I picked it up and gave one of the scuffed wheels a spin. The decal on the underside of the board was a cartoon of a skateboarder doing a handstand of sorts. His right hand was planted on the ground and his left held the skateboard to his feet, which were sticking up in the air. The trick was called a handplant, and I'd always enjoyed watching skaters who could pull it off. Two things made this picture different, however: he was handplanting on the edge of a steep cliff and, scarier yet, he was wearing a suit and tie.

I tucked the board under my arm and walked up the back stairs to the patio outside the kitchen, fished for my key, and opened the door. I made a quick call to Rich Delacroix's office and left him a message that we needed to talk first thing in the morning. I didn't want to leave the gory details on his voice mail and, more important, I wasn't yet sure what, exactly, I was going to tell him.

I walked into the living room and kicked off my shoes. Mary Ellen's pad, my WUP, lay on the end table where I'd left it, but it looked different.

Someone had doodled in it.

■ FIFTY–NINE

I tore into my WUP that night, trying to capture as much as I could of what I'd learned from that evening's discussions and events. I wrote my freedom list; I scribbled some thoughts about Cam and Agnes and Mary Ellen. I just let it roll, trying not to judge my observations, as per Smitty's explicit instructions. Several hours later, still reflecting on my daughter's Italy experience, I called and left a goodnight message on Angelica's cell phone, bolted all the doors from the inside, for obvious reasons, and threw myself into bed.

Falling asleep is usually the least of my challenges, but that night I tossed like the surf had rolled up under my bed. I chalked up the skateboard and WUP doodles to Smitty's eccentric glee in invading my apartment, so that didn't bother me too much. The day's conversations and the blowup with Cam, however, gave me a lot to think about, and my mind just wouldn't stop boiling. The morning couldn't come soon enough.

I didn't need the alarm, but I waited for it anyway. I jumped up, showered, dressed, scooped up the skateboard, and drove down to the address in Ocean Beach that Agnes had given me before I'd left her house.

There was going to be a meeting, she'd told me, that I wouldn't want to miss. "A network of extraordinary people," she'd said, who get together once a month to encourage, inspire, and cajole each other to *keep on keepin' on*, as we geezers used to say. A skate park seemed like an odd place for that kind of meeting, but that's where the address led me.

The sign over the small building said *SKATE!* in all caps and italics. I pushed through the doors and walked up to the counter. The back of the room had a giant arched doorway leading out to a large outdoor lot built up with a series of concrete and wooden ramps, rails, stairs, and small empty swimming pools. Large block letters etched on the archway formed two words that I could only assume expressed the personality and purpose of the establishment and its extreme customers:

NO POSERS

There were a couple of skaters crisscrossing each other on a giant half-pipe, a large, U-shaped ramp popular with the more accomplished skaters. I could hear the gravelly grind of wheels. They made no sounds, whoops, or yelps at all as the skaters focused to master their stunts.

I walked through the archway to get a closer look—I love to watch that stuff—but a young man with a hoop in his nose and a pin through his lip stopped me in my tracks. He wore a T-shirt with a complex, colorful pattern of dragons and knights coiled up together like intricate, braided strands.

"'Scuse me, sir," he said gently. "Are you Mr. Farber?"

"I am," I said. "But you can drop the Mr." The label makes me shudder, especially since the second I turned 40. "Farber or Steve will do just fine," I reached out my hand and he took it in a firm grip.

"Well you can call me Mr. Garcia, then," he laughed. "Agnes asked me to watch for you and bring you back to the meeting room. C'mon with me. Everyone's already here. There's plenty of coffee and some munchies back there, if you're interested."

"Always," I said and followed him through a door on the left side of the counter and into a large, modest room set with card tables and folding chairs. The seating was arranged in a large square so everyone could see each other. There were 25, maybe 30, people already sitting and listening intently to one of their peers. A few heads turned toward the door as we walked in and a man in crisp blue suit and crimson tie motioned me over to the seat on his left.

"Thanks, Mr. Garcia," I whispered to my escort, for some reason expecting that he'd be leaving, but he sat down in an empty chair and shuffled through a notebook on the table in front of him. I walked over, sat down next to Mr. Brooks Brothers, and took a quick inventory of the faces around the room.

There was no consistent theme or pattern here. Agnes, whom I saw as soon as I came in, was by far the oldest of the gaggle, and the good-natured Mr. Garcia—I'd put him at 18 or 19—was clearly the youngest. Black, white, Asian, Hispanic, Indian, male and female, young and old, sharp clothing, shorts, and sweats—this crowd was a diverse and lively mix of people who were clearly engaged and happy to be in the same room together. I was suddenly aware that a silence had settled over the gathering.

"Steve?" Agnes was asking, apparently for the second time, at least.

"Oh, I'm sorry," I said. "Hi, Agnes, everybody." I did a little embarrassed wave around the room.

"Glad you could join us," said Agnes. "I asked you to come a little bit late so I could tell the group about you before you got here, which I've already done."

Several people nodded and smiled; a few mouthed hi, hello, good morning, and the like. "I'm afraid I'm at a bit of a disadvantage, folks." I talk to groups for a living, so I'm perfectly comfortable having all eyes on me. Some would even say I prefer it. However, usually I know why I'm talking in the first place. "I'm not really sure what's... what's going on here."

Several sympathy laughs broke out around the room. I always take that as an encouraging signal. "That didn't come out right. What I mean is, Agnes told me a little about how some folks get together to support each other and all that. That's pretty much all I know. So... Agnes?"

"So... Steve?" She was playing with me.

"Mind telling me what happens now?"

"Certainly, baby, happy to. Now you get to hear from the experts about the third element of the Radical Edge. You know what I'm talkin' about."

"Yes, I do. Change the world."

"Now that," Agnes laughed, "is a mighty fine idea."

■ SIXTY

I've always wondered what it would be like to be the surprise guest on a game show like *This Is Your Life*, or to be the focus of *Extreme Makeover: Personality Edition*. Now, with the way all these people were looking at me, I had an inkling. It wasn't exactly comfortable.

"But why, if I may ask, all the attention on me? I can't possibly be the purpose of your meeting, and, well, a little context would be helpful here, I guess."

"If I may," cut in Mr. Brothers with a voice as refined as his suit. "You *are* the center of attention this morning, Steve."

"I are?"

"Yes, just as everyone in this room was in the very beginning."

"I'm sorry, the very beginning of what?" This might have been creepy if these people hadn't seemed so nice.

"All of us here," he explained, "have devoted ourselves, personally and professionally, to changing the world, in some way, for the better. We all strive to use what we have—talent, desire, resources, imagination, time—to make a difference, if I may use the cliché. To put it another way, to expand the *rightness* of things.

"We don't consider ourselves to be naïve or idealistic, although others certainly may. We are pragmatists of the highest order. We believe there is nothing more eminently practical than looking at the world, asking how can this be better? And then holding ourselves personally accountable for getting it done.

"So, what we have here, Steve, is a collection of businesspeople—some independent owners, some corporate executives, some employees, some social entrepreneurs—who all have one common desire: to help each other to help each other."

I let that settle for a moment as I looked around the room for any signs of dissonance or cynicism. I saw none, so I gathered that this sharp-dressed dude was doing a good job as spokesperson.

"What we also have here, Steve," he continued after a short pause, "is an invitation. We are inviting you to join us."

"Come again?" I said.

"Agnes gave us your background this morning. She told us a lot about you. Not everything, I'm sure, but enough for us to know that you would benefit from us," he gestured to the group, "and we, from you. If you'd care to, that is."

"Well, I'm honored, I think. But I'm not so sure what I have to bring to the... um... tables."

"I think you have a lot," Agnes chimed in. "But let us tell you what we're all about, and then you can decide. Is that fair?"

I nodded. "Sure."

"By the way," said the Suit. "I'm Ronald Perricone. I'm an executive at Maritime and Son."

My head snapped around to take him in again in a new, surprising light.

"This group, gathering, network—whatever you choose to call it—was founded many years ago by William Maritime and Agnes Golden. It started with the two of them at Agnes's diner and expanded over the years from a duo to this group that you see here today, all through personal invitation."

"Invitation based on what? How do you decide who gets to sit in the position I'm in right now?" I was also wondering about initiation or hazing rites, but I kept that to myself.

"There are no specific criteria, Steve. We don't try to quantify the kind of colleague we want; instead, we look for someone whose intent to change the world is as deep as ours is. People tend to group with others who are most like themselves, and we don't want to homogenize."

My mind flashed back to the team of Jims.

"The only similarities we look for are intent and conviction. We are interested in those who strive—and that's an important word—to change a piece of their world for the better. We're not interested in talkers; only practitioners. And there's one more critical factor."

"What's that?" I asked.

"Let me put it this way: when we get together it feels much more like a reunion than a work session. We love each other's company; therefore, we only invite people whom we're pretty sure we're going to love."

"Well... then I'm honored, I guess. I'm a loveable guy, that's true," I mugged. "But I don't know if I qualify as a practitioner."

"We think you're underestimating yourself, but let me finish telling you what we do here. Once a month we get together and compare notes about what we're seeing in the world around us and what we're trying to do in response to it."

That's when I noticed that each person around the tables had some kind of notebook, pad, or electronic gadget placed on the table in front of them. Some were yellow legal pads, others were spiral or steno books, and a few electronic tablets and assorted laptops were glowing up at their owners. They were all variations, I gathered, of the same species: they were all WUPs.

"And then," Ronald continued, "we try to come up with some solutions, some new ideas, and some breakthroughs for one another—"

"—in order to change things for the better" I added.

"Exactly," said Ronald. "And at the same time add more value to our respective businesses and bring more joy to our lives.

"Changing the world is our ultimate responsibility as Extreme Leaders, but not at the expense of the other aspects of our lives. In other words, we change the world using the vehicle of business and the instrument of our individual uniqueness."

"We're tuned in to our own frequencies," Agnes winked, making a knob turning motion with her right hand. "And we're using them to change the world. Nothing more personally thrilling and rewarding than that, now, is there?"

I took out my WUP and noticed several smiles and nods of approval.

"Good!" encouraged Ronald. "There are four change-the-world guidelines that we've agreed on so far, but we're always open to more, and I'm sure we're missing more than a few things. Let me spell them out for you."

I wrote a heading and date on the top of the page.

"The first is to define what you mean by world, and get clear on how you want that world to be different from the current reality. World doesn't have to mean the very fabric of human existence, although it certainly could be. It could be the world of your customers, neighborhood, industry or the world of one person, for that matter. You define it for yourself.

"For example, Stan over there is the CEO of an assisted-living company devoted to changing the world of senior care. When he first joined us, Stan said this:

'When a person's biggest risk is trying to get through the day without falling down, that's not a great life.' So, Stan and his team create an environment at his facilities where people in their 70s, 80s, and 90s are encouraged to take on challenges and risks. Stan is proving to his own customers that they're still capable of living lives of great adventure and meaning, and he's proving to the rest of his industry that there's a better way to do things. And, by the way, he comes down here from Vancouver every month to join us."

MY

GET

REWARD

8

Ronald went around the table and gave a quick overview of the members and their businesses. Some focused on the world of their employees, and others on the world of their particular industry and some, like my friend, Mr. Garcia, on his own neighborhood.

"Raul Garcia, over there," Ron pointed at him with a smile, "has a silk-screening shop in Mission Beach and probably sells more T-shirts than anyone along the boardwalk. He's the best salesperson you're ever going find, I'll wager. His enthusiasm is contagious, and there's no way you can walk into his shop without buying at least one shirt, and don't be surprised if you walk out with a closetful."

"One correction," said Raul. "No one who buys a shirt will ever leave with just one."

"That's pretty confident," I challenged.

"No, it's a fact," he countered. "You wanna know why?"

"You betcha," I said.

"Because if they buy one, I'm gonna give 'em another, whether they want it or not. I don't advertise that. I want my customers to advertise it for me. I want them to go home and say, *you gotta check this place out.*"

I was impressed with this young dude who obviously had *merchant* stamped all over his DNA, but I had to ask one question:

"That's very cool, Raul. But how, exactly, does that change the world?"

"It doesn't," he said. "But I got a hell of a business going, don't I?"

Everyone laughed, including me, but I knew there had to be more to it.

"Seriously, though, dude," Raul said. "I'm changing the world of my neighborhood by the way I hire my employees who are, by the way, the best salespeople in the world, next to me."

"How's that?" I asked.

"They're all homeless street kids when I first get a hold of 'em. Do you have any idea what kind of will and smarts it takes to survive on the street? I find kids with personality and drive, and I nurture it. I figure if I can channel some of that into something productive—" His voice trailed off for a moment and then picked up steam again. "Sometimes I get screwed, taken advantage of, ripped off, even, but that's the price I pay to find the ones that pay off for themselves and for me. The street is filled with unbelievable talent. I know it firsthand."

"Because?"

"Because that's where I came from, dude. Lived on the streets from the time I was 11 years old until the day someone gave me an opportunity: the guy that started the shop; the guy that retired and sold it to me on my 18th birthday; the guy that changed my world. Now that's the way I do it, too."

"Wow."

Not profound, I know, but there was really nothing else I could say.

■ SIXTY-ONE

There was no doubt that I was in the presence of greatness, but it was—how can I put this—*normal* greatness. These were not extraordinary, saintlike people. They were just totally committed to making a positive mark on the world, and, from what I could tell, they were all doing very well in their businesses. At least they felt they were. And unless you're a publicly traded company, that's good enough in my book. Even so, I knew we were just scratching the surface.

"Second guideline is," Ronald said, "act as though your every action has a direct impact on the world. In other words, you should perform every deed as if it will either improve the world or damage it."

"But, that's not true," I argued.

"I didn't say it was. I said *act* as though it were. There's no downside to that, is there? It gives us the mindset that we need to keep trying, whether anyone else is watching or not. Personal—even radical—accountability is when you do what it takes to change the world regardless of what anyone else is or isn't doing."

"That seems like an impossibly high standard," I said. "If I may," said Agnes. "It is a high standard that we may or may not be able to live up to. Nevertheless, it's also our way of reminding ourselves that none of us is isolated; none of us lives in a vacuum. And that is the truth. You can't deny this reality, sweetheart, the world already changes because of your influence. Each person you touch, each comment you make, each action you take hits a button, strikes a chord in someone else, gets them to think a thought or do something—no matter how small—that they wouldn't have done or thought if you hadn't connected with them. You have no idea how far that influence goes. It may last a split second or it may take them on an entirely new course. It may be good; it may be bad. It may be nothing more significant than the flutter of an eyelash or a fleeting feeling. But you cause *something* to happen, and that's the Lord's honest truth."

"You're not talking about the butterfly effect, are you?" I've always been leery of the loose way people tend to use the principle.

"You mean because you pick your nose in Singapore someone hits the lotto in Poughkeepsie?" asked Agnes with forced seriousness.

"That's the oversimplified way folks talk about it, yeah," I laughed.

"Oh my, who knows, baby? That's way beyond me, and that's for certain. All I'm saying is you're not alone on this planet no matter how isolated you may feel at times. So, instead, try to act like you're connected because—well, because you are."

Ronald picked up the thread from there: "Maybe your actions won't even be a blip on the cosmic radar screen, but so what? At least you'll have lived your life trying, and that's the only thing any of us has any control over; which brings us, conveniently, to the third guideline."

"Gimme one second, please," I said as I scratched some hasty notes in my WUP.

Ronald waited, checked to make sure I was ready, and then forged ahead.

"Third," he said. "Don't judge yourself based on the outcome of your efforts."

"Meaning?"

"Meaning you cannot ultimately control the end results. You do everything you can, you do your homework and your research, and you enlist the people you need to get the job done, whatever it is. Whether it's senior care, selling T-shirts, or coaching people to be better leaders, whatever it is you're trying to do. You define world, you get clear on how you want that world to change, you act as though all of your actions will make it happen, and then... then sometimes you succeed and sometimes you bomb, or maybe it's somewhere in between, But in any case, you never, ever judge yourself based on the outcome. If you succeed, you don't take credit for it; if you fail, you don't blame yourself. The only thing you take credit for is the fact that you tried."

I flashed back to last night's fiasco at Agnes's house. I'd wanted desperately to take credit for a miraculous transformation in the life of Cam Summerfield, I now saw. Moreover, I blamed myself for not making it happen. *I have a little work to do on guideline number three*, I thought.

"Like I said before, these are just guidelines, and there are, we're sure, a lot more where they came from. They're simple in concept and remarkably hard to practice, but that's what we're doing, practicing."

"But you said there were four," I remembered. "What's the last one?"

"Never—never, *ever*—" he resonated, "try to do it alone."

■ SIXTY-TWO

Just then, the door flew open and banged against the wall behind where Raul was sitting. We all jumped in our seats as a large, matronly-looking woman with bright red hair and a billowing, flowered summer dress heaved into the room as if she'd broken the offensive line and was making for the quarterback.

"Yow! I am so sorry, folks," she huffed. "That damn door always does that and I don't never seem to learn. I am so sorry I'm late but we had a little incident on the rail.

Some little guy was grindin' a rail from the top of the stairs and did himself a little straddle ride, if you get the picture. He won't be singing baritone for a while, if you know what I mean."

She walked around the table, came directly over to me, and thrust out a meaty hand. "I'm Carolina Jones," she bellowed. "I own this place and glad to say so, liability insurance and all!"

I laughed and gladly took her hand in mine; I liked her immediately.

"I am so sorry to interrupt the festivities." I loved the way she apologized about everything—I could just hear her saying *I am so sorry for the terrible weather,* or *I am so sorry for the wart on your nostril.* "But, I have to steal Mr. Farber here for just a sec or two."

"You do?" I said. "Is there something wrong?"

"No, no! I am so sorry to have concerned you. It's nothing like that but," she clamped her hand around my elbow and leaned in close to my ear, "I do have to borrow you."

She all but yanked me to my feet and I bleated, "be right back," to the folks as she hustled me out the door.

"Don't know if he'll be back today or not, actually," she called over her shoulder. "I am so sorry about this, folks." This time she didn't sound like she'd meant it.

"What's going on?" I pleaded as she ushered me toward the archway leading out to the ramps.

We stepped out onto the lot and she pointed to the top of the half-pipe. Just as I looked up I saw someone execute a perfect handplant, pausing for a brief moment with feet and board in the air before arching around, landing his board back on the ramp and skating back down into the U and up the other side. A helmet and pads hid the skater well, but I could still tell that he was no kid. Oddly, something about him looked familiar. I watched him repeat the same stunt over and over, perfecting the move a little more on each pass.

"I opened this place about three years ago," said Carolina. "I wanted our kids to have a safe place to skate. A place where they could help each other learn all the fine skills and characteristics that a great skater needs without worry about the, well, seedier elements of the streets. I watch out for them, try to keep them from hurting themselves too much, and fix them up when they do. Some of these kids have broken families, some are pretty well off, but when they're here, I'm the mama."

"Very cool," I said, watching the guy on the ramp. "But obviously it's not just kids that come here."

"No, it's not just kids." She put her fingers to her lips and whistled like a pro. "He's no kid, but he's an important part of the spirit of this place."

The skater looked our way and came to a stop by sliding on his knees to the bottom of the U. He kicked up his board, grabbed it in his hand, and set it down on the asphalt as he walked toward us. When he pulled off his helmet, I saw him clearly and realized with a start why he looked so familiar. He broke into a run, thumped into me with arms wide open, and clasped them around me in a great bear hug.

"Dude!" he shouted into my left ear. "It's awesome to see you! Really, really awesome!"

We pushed back from each other and I caught my breath.

"Edg! Jeez, man, what are you doing here?"

He looked as fit and lively as the last time I'd seen him, two years earlier. His goatee showed a little more salt in the pepper, and his hair was cropped to Marine length, a good look for him. His requisite Hawaiian shirt was patterned with large, colorful blooms and his baggy, khaki pants billowed out from a waist even slimmer than I remembered.

"Had a little business to take care of, so I thought I'd come over to the mainland and do it in the flesh—give myself a chance to reconnect with some old buds."

"I just wanted to see the look on your face, Steve," laughed Carolina. "And it was worth it, I must say! I thought I was gonna have to practice my CPR on you. I'll leave you two to catch up. I need to at least make an appearance at that meeting I'm supposed to be hosting." She waved and thundered back into the building.

Edg looked toward the parking lot. "You still have that Mustang of yours?"

"I sure do, Edg. She's still got a few miles on her."

"Well, then," he raised his eyebrows like the rascal that he was. "Let's blow this boneyard. We've got a lot to talk about, don't we?"

Yeah, we did, but that would have to wait. There was something I had to take care of first.

■ SIXTY-THREE

Rich Delacroix greeted me in the ILGI reception area, and we walked back to his office in silence. He said something to his assistant, followed me into his office, and shut the door behind us. He perched himself on the edge of his large, slate desktop and I stood facing him with my hands in my pockets.

"I want you to know, Rich, that I really tried," I began without his asking me to. "I spent the day with Cam, even introduced him to some pretty sharp folks who all—out of the goodness of their hearts, mind you—were more than willing to share their knowledge with him. Just to help him out, you know?"

He nodded, so I pressed on.

"I don't want to say anything inappropriate, and I don't want to put this all on Cam, so let's just say that he and I just don't click. I have to admit that I was a little disappointed with myself, but, hey, it is what it is, and I'm clearly not the guy to work with him..."

The words ran out.

"I hope you understand, Rich."

"I do," he said simply.

"So, if I may ask, what happens with Cam now?"

"It's already happened," he said and pressed a button on his phone. "Ask her to come in now, please," he said into the speaker.

Spunky was the first word that popped into my brain when I saw her. She wore a navy dress suit and carried a black leather-covered notebook, which added to her sharp, professional mien.

"I'm Lisa Appleman," she said, not waiting for an introduction. We shook hands, and I must have cocked my head, or knitted my brow or done something to indicate that I didn't comprehend, because she quickly followed up with, "I'm the new SVP of sales."

Rich and I looked at each other.

"That was fast," I said.

"Yeah, it was," said Rich. "But it didn't happen the way you think."

"Do you want to tell me about it?" I asked, hoping that he would.

"He wasn't fired," said Lisa in a compassionate voice that took me by surprise.

"And I didn't exactly demote him, either," added Rich.

"What do you mean, *exactly?*" I said. "Seems to me that you either did or you didn't."

"What I mean," Rich started to explain, "is that I didn't demote Cam."

Now I was really lost. "Well, who did, then?"

"Cam did."

I shook my head. "Not following you."

"Cam came in early this morning and said he'd been thinking all night after spending the day, and apparently part of the evening, with you and your *friends*, he called them."

I did not want to rehash last night's discussion, so I kept quiet, for once.

"He said he realized that managing other people wasn't for him, at least for right now, and that he'd much rather just get back on the phones and sell. He was itching to break his own personal best sales records. He offered to relinquish his title immediately and asked if I'd let him keep his office so he could work without distraction and *burn it up*. So, what could I say? He gave us all the perfect solution, because—I'll be honest with you, Steve—that's exactly what I was going to offer him. Well, that or a severance package."

"Much better this way, though, isn't it?" I couldn't fight back a smile.

"Much," said Lisa. "He's on my team; I can't wait to see what he does. I'm going to do everything I can to support him."

Now, that's what I'm talkin' about, I thought. "Well, Lisa, if you ever need any help with him..." I began.

"Yes?"

"Well... I may want another crack at him, is all."

"Thanks," she said. "I'll remember that."

Yeah, I thought. *So will I.*

■ SIXTY-FOUR

I must have made a wrong turn as I walked down the hallway away from Rich's office. I thought reception would be on my right, but, instead, I was looking at a row of offices I'd never seen before. In an attempt to get my bearings I glanced around and *bam!* there he was in the office across the way.

Cam was working like a vortex: he had a phone on one ear and a headset wrapped around the other. An assistant was sitting in a chair next to his desk, sliding files in front of him as he talked into the mouthpiece in soft, rapid tones.

I tried to scoot on past without him seeing me, but he suddenly looked up and waved me in without missing a beat of rhythm on the phone. I heard him ask the person to hold, and he jabbed the button like a prizefighter.

"Farber," he said in a rush. "Sorry, you know, about last night. About the whole day. I know you think you wasted your time."

"Yeah, well, don't worry about it, Cam. I really do wish you great success; I hope you knock 'em dead." Okay, so it was a cliché.

"You didn't, though," he said as he took his call off hold.

"I didn't what?" I stage whispered, but as far as he was concerned, I was already gone. I gave a little wave, which he didn't see, and started to turn toward the door. That's when I saw it, lying open on the desk next to his stack of files.

Cam's Wake-Up Pad.

Déjà Vu

It was another one of those typical San Diego days: the sky was blue and bright, and the ocean was sparkling as it slapped its waves onto the shores of Mission Beach. I was sitting on the seawall, lost in thought and filled with a new sense of—what was it?—optimism, I guess.

It made my day, seeing that pad on Cam's desk. Something had stuck, and it was no small thing at that. I was actually impressed with his decision to give up management and go back on the phones. That took some kind of guts. Most people would have quit and gone in search of a new place, but he chose to stay and become a champion all over again, and this time he'd be doing what really trips his trigger. Come to think of it, I think Cam may just have found his frequency.

So I had to wonder, maybe Cam's world had changed a little, but did that qualify me as a change the world practitioner? I decided I wasn't ready to claim that, exactly, but it sure felt like progress. Best of all, after my exposure to the WUP, my conversations with Agnes, and the guidelines from the gathering at *SKATE!*, I felt that I had something tangible and helpful to bring back to the Jims on my next trip to Michigan.

Not only that, but maybe I'd learned a few things that could be worthy of my adding to Edg and Pops' *Daily Handbook for Extreme Leaders*. Honestly, I'd never thought that would happen.

I was jolted out of my musings by a sudden, sloppy lick on the side of my face. A jumbo-sized Golden Retriever had come up behind the seawall and ambushed me with a kiss.

"Sadie! How you doin', you big poochie?" I gave her a mighty scratch behind her ears.

Since Smitty had been house-sitting for Edg and taking care of Sadie for the last couple of years, I knew that the boys had to be close by. I spun around on the seawall, jumped down onto the boardwalk, and scanned the area.

I'd already realized that Edg's reappearance hadn't been as sudden as I'd thought. He'd been back in San Diego for a while without my knowing it.

His baby, XinoniX, the company he'd founded and retired from, was looking at an acquisition, and he'd come to town to help with the due diligence process. When Janice told him about my new coaching engagement, Edg started doing what he does best.

He helped me without my knowing it.

However, not at the expense of the fathomless joy he takes in messing with my head.

He wrote the note the same morning that Smitty had given it to me; he set up the lunch with Agnes and then came by the diner to spy on us. That's when he paid the tab. He got into my apartment, left his skateboard in my garage, and scribbled in my Wake-Up Pad just for fun. The guy delights in seeing me twist, squirm, lurch, writhe, and all the other words that you'll find in the thesaurus under struggle. In other words, he gets deep satisfaction in watching me try to come to terms with myself.

Do you have any idea how that makes me feel?

Like the luckiest human being on the planet.

A Daily Handbook
for Extreme Leaders:

How to Do What You Love in the Service of People Who Love What You Do

By William G. Maritime and Son
(With additions by Steve Farber, at the request of the original authors)

■ SET UP YOUR WUP

Choose a notebook or tablet—paper or electronic—to use as your first Wake-Up Pad and write these headings as a reminder of how to use it:

Scan & Eavesdrop

Skim the bestseller lists, magazine racks, television listings, and headlines of newspapers from around the country and the world. Scope out the room that you're sitting in and the crowd that you're walking with. Watch the trends in technology. Be an anthropologist. Study behavior. Notice things. Scan.

Listen to what people are saying at work, at home, in the supermarket, on the radio. What are your customers saying about their own challenges in their work? What are your neighbors saying about theirs? Did you hear something noteworthy? Don't judge; record.

Ponder

Review what you've seen and heard. Now ask yourself: What do these things mean to me and mine? What are the implications for and the impact on my business, my life, the world? What other questions do I need to ask about what I've seen and heard?

Also ask: What's most important in my life? Why? What's my frequency? How do I consistently live in tune with it? What, if anything, is missing?

This is your space to consider anything—anything at all. Don't edit, don't judge; just reflect, and let it roll.

Talking Points

Recruit a team of fellow Extreme Leaders: your team at work, your fellow volunteers in your community efforts, your family, neighbors, and friends. Choose a time and place to gather, talk, kick it around, commiserate, and conspire; a time to compare notes on your experiences as human beings.

List the things you want to bring to the group's attention, the things you find interesting, funny, odd, inspiring; the things you need help understanding. The things you find noteworthy.

Try This

Now that you've scanned, eavesdropped, pondered for a while, and talked about it with some trusted kindred spirits, it's time to do something. Do something bold, something audacious. Something that could change the world for the better.

These are the things I'm going to experiment with...

These are the things I'll change right now...

These are the commitments I make to the
people around me and to myself...

These are the people I'll need to help get it all done...

Now that your WUP is primed and ready to go, keep it handy as you explore the following pages and use it to capture your thoughts, ideas and plans because you're going to have a lot to ponder, to talk about, to try.

You, my friend, are about to take a Radical Leap forward.

■ CULTIVATE LOVE

Love is the ultimate motivation of the Extreme Leader: love of something or someone, love of a cause, love of a principle, love of the people you work with and the customers you serve, love of the future you and yours can create together, love of the business you conduct together every day.

Think about it...

Without the calling and commitment of your heart, there's no good reason for you to take a stand, to take a risk, to do what it takes to change your world for the better.

Think about it...

You take your heart to work with you every day, and so does everyone else—everyone, that is, who falls into the general category of human being. So, think about it. Right now. Answer the following questions for yourself. Take some time; think it through. Write your answers in your WUP. Once you're clear on the answer, tell people. That's right, you need, ultimately, to answer these questions out loud—and often—to the people you aspire to lead.

"Why do I love this business, this company?"

(Answer out loud, please.)

"Why do I love this project, this idea, this system, this procedure, this policy?"

(Answer out loud, please.)

"Why do I love my customers?"

(Answer out loud, please.)

Then answer this question, not with words but through your actions:

"How will I show that love in the way I work with, serve, and lead the people around me?"

Here are a couple of powerful ways to do that:

1. Cultivate Your Fascination

Take a Story Inventory

Think of the people you encounter at work as either internal or external to your business. Write down the names of one or two key internal people—colleagues, employees, staff, managers, partners, associates, et cetera. Write down the name(s) of one or two key external people—customers, vendors, suppliers, et cetera.

Now list everything you know about each person beyond the function he or she serves. Assess how much you know or don't know about each as a human being.

Ask each person to tell you one important story or event from his or her life. Look for an opportunity to find out more during your next conversation. Ask each to share with you his or her number one business challenge. Ask if there's some way you can be of service—something you can do to help with each person's challenge. Even if that person declines your offer, he or she will always appreciate your asking.

Now pick one to two more people and do it again. Repeat until you run out of people—for the rest of your life, in other words.

2. Express Your Gratitude

Write a Professional Love Note

At least once a day, write a personal, handwritten note of appreciation, thanks, or recognition:

1. Think about a specific person at work.
2. List that person's finest qualities and/or greatest achievements.
3. Reflect on why you appreciate those qualities and achievements.
4. Write the note.
5. Give the note.

Make it a habit, not an assignment. In other words, always write from your heart and express your sincere appreciation. The note bridges words with action. You're demonstrating love through the act of writing and delivering it.

But don't do this because you have to; do it because you want to.

So, *want to.*

You are now in the business of cultivating love. And watch, just watch, how love comes back to you wrapped beautifully in the words and actions of others.

The bottom line: Love is good business. Customers who love you will return to you, your product, your service, and your company. Employees who love you will bring themselves fully into their work day after day, no matter that the company down the street is paying a bit more.

Love is your retention strategy.

So, how do you get them to love you? Simple, really,

Go first...

or don't bother calling yourself leader, let alone Extreme Leader.

■ GENERATE ENERGY

Energy 1: internal or inherent power; capacity of acting, operating, or producing an effect **2:** strength of expression; force of utterance; power to impress the mind and arouse the feelings; life; spirit

—American Heritage and Webster's dictionaries

The Extreme Leader is a generator, a powerful force for action, for progress, and an enthusiastic believer in people and in their capacity to do the awesome.

What gets you out of bed and brings you into work? If you are to be the generator, where does *your* juice come from? In what well do you dip your cup to get the nourishment you need to meet the obstacles and challenges that you and yours face every day? Find out and go there often.

Make a list of your personal energizers and encourage others to do the same.

The answers are different for each of us, certainly, but there are some universal sources of energy that are available to all.

Don't worry, this isn't esoteric; it's not metaphysics—not that there's anything wrong with that.

So, what generates energy?

- Love
- Great ideas
- Noble principles
- Leaping goals
- Interesting work
- Exciting challenges
- Compelling vision of the future

That's a pretty good start. If you're doubtful, consider the opposite: Imagine working at a place you hate, a place that squashes ideas, ignores principles, sets goals you can accomplish in a coma, provides boring work, provides no challenge, and has no idea where it's going in the future—actually, it doesn't matter that they don't know where they're going, because a company like that will never get there anyway.

Feeling energized yet? Of course not. For you, the Extreme Leader, the ultimate test will be:

"What effect does my action have on the energy of the people around me?"

Experiment with some of these:

Remember/discover why you're here.

Are you just filling in time between weekends? No? Then answer this:

"What is your work really all about? What is your higher purpose?"

Tell people. Ask them for their help in living up to that purpose.

Encourage great ideas from people.

Never assume that an idea is stupid just because it sounds that way to you. Your response: Go try it. *If it doesn't work, ask:*

"What's the lesson for you and us?"

Stand on principle; work for a cause.

Principles and values are there to guide your actions and decisions. They are the standard. But consider this:

The Extreme Leader doesn't just meet the existing standards; she or he defines higher ones.

So...

What are your noble principles and values?

Nail them on the wall. *Tell everyone, everywhere you go:*

"This is what's important around here. Judge me by my ability to live up to them."

Now you're working for a cause, not just a paycheck.

Set leap goals.

Your goals should require that you leap and experience OS!Ms to meet them, not stretch, as some have said. A leap goal will *require* you to get excited and energetic if you're going to make it. Set goals that tap into the talents, skills, hopes, and aspirations of your team and company, and people will generate the energy necessary to leap up and hit those goals.

"What goals can you set for your team and your company today that will tap into the talents, skills, hopes, and aspirations of your people?"

Purge the suckers.

Get rid of the energy suckers. Encourage people to root out and discard any work that hinders your cause.

Ask yourself; ask your people:

"What are the unnecessary, time-consuming, bureau-cratic policies and procedures that suck our energy?"

"What are we doing that keeps us from fulfilling our and our customers' goals and dreams?"

"What should we change in order to make this a more interesting, exciting, scintillating, and awesome place to work?"

Connect human-to-human.

Communicate yourself, your humanity. Don't just recite your company's vision statement, talk in your own words. Talk to people about your ideas for the future, and ask for theirs. Be the person that you are.

Forget your title, forget your position, and speak from your heart.

Talk not only of your hopes for the future but also about your foibles today. Vulnerability aids human connection, and connection is the conduit for energy. Pretense of invincibility builds walls and creates distance between human hearts.

Find Your Frequency and Amp it Up

Tune in to your frequency. List five values or principles that are most important to you in the way you live your life. Write down your best definition of each value. It only has to make sense to you.

Read through your list and your definitions. Now tune in to one by considering the following perspectives. Which *one* of these values—

—is the most important to you in the way you live your life?

—has the clearest meaning for you?

—feels the best?

—most accurately describes who you really are?

—best describes how you'd like others to know you?

—most fully encompasses your other values?

—energizes you when you think about it?

—if it were a radio station, would you turn up the loudest?

That's your frequency.

Amp it up. Think of all the roles you play in your life at work, at home, in the community, and with your family and friends. To what degree do you live by your frequency in each of those roles? In other words, at what volume does your frequency play in each role?

For the next week, take notes in your WUP about how your frequency shows up—or doesn't—in your activities in the roles you play. Then work on the solution(s) to this question:

What can you change about your activities, your attitude, your priorities, or your choices that will bring you more in tune with your frequency and reduce the static in your life?

If you're more of a visual person, you can use these frequency worksheets to help you focus your thinking:

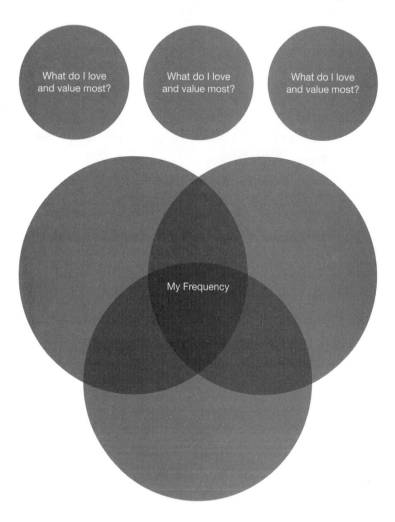

In the circles, list the things you love and value most, then see where they overlap. This could be your frequency.

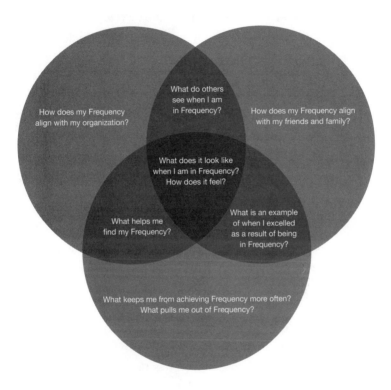

■ INSPIRE AUDACITY

For the Extreme Leader, audacity is a bold and blatant disregard for normal constraints in order to change the world for the better. Love-inspired audacity is courageous and filled with valor. The Extreme Leader is audacious not to serve his or her own ego, but to serve the common good. And to do so boldly and blatantly and let the naysayers be damned.

Watch out...

The most common and insidious normal constraints are the ones that are imposed on you by others. This imposition is not malicious, necessarily. It just comes from a sad, limited set of beliefs about what's possible.

Don't let their beliefs become yours.

Normal constraints take many forms. Whenever you have an idea, whenever you see a better way to do things or better things to do, make a list of all the normal constraints that seem to be holding you back. Are they systems, policies, or procedures? Is it a particular person or group of people? Do you doubt yourself? Is your company's history holding you back? Many audacious ideas and actions have been thwarted by the simple words: "We tried that once, and it didn't work then," or "That'll never work around here; it's just not the way we do it," or "You're dreaming."

Now, for the all the right reasons, disregard that list!

And then ask and answer the following question. It is the ultimate audacity question because of its scope and extraordinary possibilities. *It is impossible to be an Extreme Leader without putting this question at the center of your agenda:*

"How are we going to change the world?"

You can tackle that by thinking, literally, about the entire world, the global community. And bless you for thinking that way. By the same token, however, it is no less noble to ask and answer this question:

"How are we going to change the world of our company, employees, customers, marketplace, and industry?"

Remember, the entire world is made up solely of people like the ones you touch in your personal and professional life. So, why not start with your world? Every normal constraint in the proverbial book will tell you that this question is unrealistic and a waste of time. Boldly and blatantly disregard that book.

Now ask others to join you in this endeavor. Show them what you think is possible, and show them that your belief in their capabilities is greater than their belief in their own. Ask others to help you to change the world and you have just inspired audacity.

And to help you get started in this noble endeavor, courtesy of Ronald Perricone and his team, here are the

Four SKATE! Guidelines for Changing the World

1. What is your world—the world you'd like to change?

- Who is in it?
- What is your relationship to these individuals?
- Why do you care about them?
- Why do you care so deeply about this world?
- How do you want your world to be different than it is today? Be specific about what changes need to happen and what a changed world will look like in the future.

"Act as if your every action has a direct impact on the world. In other words, perform every deed as if it will either improve the world or damage it."

—Ronald Perricone and SKATE!

2. List the first three steps you personally need to take in order to create the change you described.

1.
2.
3.

Set a deadline for Step #1. If the above quote were literally true, what would you do differently starting right now?

"Don't judge yourself based on the outcome of your efforts.
If you succeed, don't take credit for it;
if you fail, don't blame yourself.
The only thing you take credit for
is the fact that you tried."

—Ronald Perricone and SKATE!

3. Write the above quote on a piece of paper and tape it to your bathroom mirror.

Now, review #2 and get going.

"Never—never, ever—try to do it alone."

—Ronald Perricone and SKATE!

4. Build your own SKATE! Team and create your community for change.

Consider starting with one or two others and grow from there. Take your time finding like-minded people who want to change their worlds for the better and who fully believe that, with help, they can get it done. These are people you'd love to spend time with, people who are different from you, yet whose frequencies are harmonious with your own. Most importantly, build a team of people who can contribute to one another.

Experiment and find the best structure for your meetings. Whatever works for you will be the right way. Try this meeting process:

1. Take turns reading new entries from your WUPs.
2. Have an open, no holds barred conversation about your findings and observations.
3. Give a progress report on each person's change the world project and identify areas that need help, ideas, or solutions.
4. Brainstorm ideas and solutions, as a group, for each project.
5. Take a few minutes of solo time to record notes in your WUPs.

■ PROVIDE PROOF

Are you really an Extreme Leader? Prove it.

Prove it through the alignment between your words and your actions. Prove it by standing up for what's right. Prove it through measurable, tangible signs of progress. Prove it through your own experience. Prove it through your phenomenal successes. Prove it through your glorious failures. And prove it all on these three levels:

1. Prove it to others.
2. Prove it to yourself.
3. Prove to others that you're proving it to yourself.

Prove it to others.

It's been called a lot of things over the years: *walk your talk; practice what you preach; put your money where your mouth is; set the example.* Jim Kouzes and Barry Posner said it best: DWYSYWD. Dwi-zee-wid. Do What You Say You Will Do.

Whenever humanly possible make sure that your actions and behaviors live up to and reflect the words and ideas, promises, and commitments that come out of your mouth.

Ask yourself:

"What have I done today that shows my commitment to my colleagues and customers?"

"How have I changed the World/world, even a little bit, today? What measurable, tangible evidence can I provide?"

"What will I do tomorrow to demonstrate the power of my convictions?"

Prove it to yourself.

The OS!M is the natural, built in indicator that you are quite possibly fully engaged in the act of Extreme Leadership. Pursue it, it's your internal barometer that you're moving in the right direction. This is not about fear for fear's sake; it's not about the adrenaline rush just for the thrill of it. This is about the fear and thrill that are part and parcel of the leadership experience. It's the fear and thrill that we experience in the process of attempting the awesome, the extraordinary. It's how you prove it to yourself. There is no Extreme Leadership without the OS!M.

Do you think you've empowered someone? Did it scare you? Did you have an OS!M as you thought about what that person might do with his or her newfound discretion? If not, you haven't pushed it far enough. Increase the scope of the empowerment until you feel it in your gut, even if you have to push it to a million dollar spending authority. Feel the OS!M now? Good. That's growth.

Reflect in your WUP...

"What are the OS!Ms in my past that resulted in my being where I am today? What lessons did I learn in those OS!Ms that I should continue to apply?"

And if you could do them over...

"What would I keep the same in spite of a particular failure? What would I change in spite of a particular success?"

Now...

"What potential leadership opportunity is coming up at work or at home that I can turn into my next OS!M? How will I do it?"

Prove to others that you're proving it to yourself.

Extreme Leadership is not a solo act; it doesn't happen in a vacuum. You're not going to change the world by yourself. It's your job to recruit, cultivate, and develop the Extreme Leaders in your midst. This is nothing new. You've heard it before: develop people. True, true, and true again.

However...

The most overlooked way to develop Extreme Leadership in others is to let them participate in *your* development. *You* be the living, breathing example of a work in progress.

That's what we all are anyway, right? Say to them, "Watch me try." Give others the benefits of your OS!Ms.

That's right...

Pursue your OS!Ms in full, public view.

Show others that you're learning, you're trying, you're botching it up from time to time. Then let them in on what you've learned.

Guess what will happen?

They'll try, too. You've proven to others that you're proving it to yourself. They'll want to prove it to themselves, too.

But don't leave it there. Invite them to share in your development directly.

Seek extreme feedback. Ask these questions:

"What do I need to do to improve as an Extreme Leader? Where am I screwing up? How can I get better?"

Don't give up until you get their answers—until you've proven that you mean it.

Extreme Leader Action Plan

I will change the World/world by:

- Why is this important to me (Frequency)?

- How will this be important to my team/organization?

- How will it make the World/world better?

- Who will I involve in generating Energy for this change? What about this change will energize them? What will they need to help lead this change?

What will this change look like?

- What Energy Suckers will need to be purged/ minimized in order to initiate and sustain this change? How will I mitigate them?

- What OS!Ms must I pursure to facilitate this change? What fears do I have with pursuing this goal?

- How will I show my commitment to this change? To others? To myself?

■ ACKNOWLEDGMENTS

My endless admiration and humble gratitude go out to the amazing folks who continue to inspire me to do what I love in the service of people who love what I do. For example:

To Todd Sattersten for his sparkling knowledge of the business book world and his invaluable guidance and encouragement on this project.

To Steve Dealph and Joanne Brooks, who started out as "fans" and ended up as the driving force behind the design and launch of The Extreme Leadership Workshop.

To Tommy Spaulding, my dear and immensely talented friend who's proven that the GTY Project goes both ways.

To Chris Snook, Jeremy Brown, Kandi Miller, Christine Whitmarsh, Paige Schwahn, and Ryan Anderson of the No Limit Publishing team for bringing a level of drive and creativity that is virtually unheard of in the traditional publishing universe.

To Holli Catchpole, Cassie Glasgow, Michele Rubino, Marsha Horshok, Jenny Canzoneri, and Kim Stark of the Speakers Office team who manage my speaking calendar and tolerate my warped sense of humor daily.

To Burton Goldfield, Jimmy Franzone and the TriNet Team whose partnership enabled this book to come together when it did. Ambition realized!

To my educator friends David Pinter, Glen Warren, Jim Wipke, Jill Schuelen, Angela Maiers, Debby Granger, Chris Corliss, Laura Philyaw, Eric Pearson, Jim Thomas, and Mike McDonough, whose stalwart belief that this work can change the world of education convinced me to believe the same.

To Travis Collier, who helps keep @stevefarber on Twitter populated with links to fantastic leadership content.

To Simon Billsberry, the smartest entrepreneur I've ever known, and his award-winning team at Kineticom, a company that exemplifies the principles of Extreme Leadership in every fabric of their culture.

To my sons, Saul and Jeremy, daughter, Angelica, and steppies, Kelsey, Heather and Presley, who make me proud to be a father and stepfather; to my brother, Bill Farber, and sister, Mary Platt, who know what energy and love are and how to use them to help others.

And, as always, to my wife and partner, Veronica (you can call her Nikki, if you prefer), whose tender, compassionate heart and life-affirming spirit nurture my own capacity to love.

■ ABOUT THE AUTHOR

Steve Farber is the president of Extreme Leadership, Inc. and the founder of The Extreme Leadership Institute, organizations devoted to changing the world through the cultivation and development of Extreme Leaders in the business community, non-profits, and education. Former vice president and official mouthpiece—that's what it said on his business card—of The Tom Peters Company, Farber is a seasoned leadership coach and consultant who has worked with a vast array of public and private organizations in virtually every arena, from the tech sector to financial services, manufacturing, healthcare, hospitality, entertainment, retail, public education, non-profits, and government.

He's the author of *Greater Than Yourself: The Ultimate Lesson of True Leadership*, which debuted as a *USA Today* and *Wall Street Journal* bestseller, and his first book, *The Radical Leap: A Personal Lesson in Extreme Leadership*, was named as one of the 100 Best Business Books of All Time.

He lives, as you may have guessed, in the San Diego area.

Bring Steve Farber or his team to your next meeting or conference and develop Extreme Leaders in your organization

Steve personally delivers dynamite **keynotes** and intensive half-day or full-day workshops for companies and associations around the globe. He also accepts a small handful of clients for personal **coaching**. For more information or to contact Steve directly, please visit *www.stevefarber.com* or email *info@stevefarber.com*.

The Extreme Leadership Institute provides **training, certification, consulting, and coaching** based on Steve Farber's approaches and methodologies. For more information on **The Extreme Leadership Workshop: Taking the Radical Leap** and other remarkable offerings, please visit *www.ExtremeLeadership.com*.